Elements
of
Visual Design
in the
Landscape

Other Titles From E & FN Spon

Amenity Landscape Management
A resources handbook
R. Cobham

Countryside Management
P. Bromley

Elements of Architecture
From form to place
P. von Meiss

The Idea of Building
S. Groak

Shopping Centre Design
N. K. Scott

Spon's Grounds Maintenance Contract Handbook
R. M. Chadwick

Spon's Landscape Contract Manual
A guide to good practice and procedures in the management of
landscape contracts
H. Clamp

*For more information about these and other titles published by us please
contact:* The Promotion Department, E & FN Spon, 2–6 Boundary
Row, London SE1 8HN.

Elements
of
Visual Design
in the
Landscape

Simon Bell

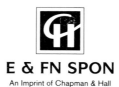

E & FN SPON
An Imprint of Chapman & Hall

London · Glasgow · New York · Tokyo · Melbourne · Madras

Published by E & FN Spon, an imprint of Chapman & Hall, 2–6 Boundary Row, London SE1 8HN

Chapman & Hall, 2–6 Boundary Row, London SE1 8HN, UK

Blackie Academic & Professional, Wester Cleddens Road, Bishopbriggs, Glasgow G64 2NZ, UK

Chapman & Hall Inc., 29 West 35th Street, New York NY10001, USA

Chapman & Hall Japan, Thomson Publishing Japan, Kirakawacho Nemoto Building, 6F, 1-7-11 Hirakawa-cho, Chiyoda-ku, Tokyo 102, Japan

Chapman & Hall Australia, Thomas Nelson Australia, 102 Dodds Street, South Melbourne, Victoria 3205, Australia

Chapman & Hall India, R. Seshadri, 32 Second Main Road, CIT East, Madras 600 035, India

First edition 1993

© 1993 Simon Bell

Designed by Geoffrey Wadsley
Typeset in United Kingdom by Keyset Composition, Colchester, Essex
Printed and bound in Hong Kong

ISBN 0 419 17590 3

A catalogue record for this book is available from the British Library

Library of Congress Cataloging-in-Publication data available

Bell, Simon.
    Elements of visual design in the landscape / Simon Bell. –– 1st
  ed.
      p.   cm.
    Includes index.
    ISBN 0-442-31649-6
    1. Landscape design.   I. Title
  SB472.45.B45   1993   92-31146
  712'.2––dc20   CIP

Contents

—— Acknowledgements ——

Since this book would not have come to fruition unless the original structure upon which it is based had been put together and honed down by my former colleagues Duncan Campbell and Oliver Lucas, it is to them that I owe my greatest debt of thanks. The large number of people, especially staff of the Forestry Commission, who have been taught design principles along the lines presented in this book deserve thanks for their unwitting role as guinea pigs over the years. They are too numerous to mention but they have never been able to look at the landscape in the same way since!

A special word of thanks is also due to the Forestry Commission who gave me permission to use a good deal of material in their possession, particularly the vast majority of the photographs used in the book.

Staff at the Canadian Museum of Civilization and Douglas Cardinal, Architects, assisted me with plans and information useful in the first case study while Sarah Slazenger at Powerscourt helped me over the details of the second case study; I am very grateful to them.

Last, but not least, my family have been exceptionally patient, my wife Jacquie most particularly, since it was she who slaved over a hot word processor and at times had to decipher my handwriting. Thank you all.

Preface

The professions working in the countryside – foresters, land agents, engineers – are practical people well versed in the functional side of their work but perhaps not so comfortable when it comes to dealing with visual issues. I believe that it is increasingly important to be able to discuss and use visual design principles in a rational and structured way. The catalogue of principles is not entirely new, being familiar to architects, landscape architects and urban designers, but there is a need to extend their application from built or predominantly urban environments into the wider landscape where three dimensions are more important, where the scale is bigger and where natural patterns and processes predominate over man-made ones.

The origins of this book lie in work carried out by my colleagues and myself as the first landscape architects employed by the Forestry Commission, the British forestry service. Following Duncan Campbell's lead in 1975 we have developed the means of designing man-made forests, largely in the open, semi-natural upland landscapes of Britain. We recognized early on that in order for forest managers to achieve an adequate understanding of the landscapes they are working in from a visual as well as functional point of view, they require an appreciation of the components of the existing landscape and how they fit together to form patterns. From this follows an understanding of how an analysis of those patterns can be used in a creative way when planting or managing a forest.

I have been involved for some years now in providing training and advice on landscape design to all the professions involved in forest and countryside management, urban forest and park design. So successful has this method been that other organizations – the Countryside Commission, the Scottish Natural Heritage Agency, the Danish Forest and Nature Agency, the Northern

Irish Forestry Service, the Irish Forestry Board, and the US Forest Service (North West Pacific Region) – have all made use of aspects of the structure in courses or seminars I and my colleagues have run for them on behalf of the Forestry Commission. Interest in the techniques has also been shown by other organizations to whom we have lectured. In addition regular exposure to landscape and forestry students at a number of universities in Britain and abroad has demonstrated the more general need for such an approach.

Although the method was originally developed with forests in mind it was obvious from the beginning that the whole approach can be applied equally to any landscape and at any scale. The book has been illustrated using a wide range of examples from every field of landscape, architecture and urban design in order to broaden its appeal. I hope that it will provide designers and non-designers alike, both students and practising professionals, with a common language of aesthetics so that better and more informed discussions about proposals for the future visual management of our environment can be made.

Simon Bell MIC For, ALI
Dunbar

Foreword

Simon Bell has delved deeply into the philosophy and practice of landscape architecture. As landscape architect to the Forestry Commission he has had the opportunity to see landscape architecture in the wide scale of the countryside as a whole and to explore the practicality of applying landscape principles to the problems of production. More and more, landscape architecture is facing the task of reconciling production, whether in forestry or agriculture, with the creation or conservation of a landscape as sympathetic to the needs of native wildlife as to the pleasure of people.

Fortunately, in recent years the landscape profession has applied itself to an ever-increasing degree to the reconciliation of men's activities with the welfare of the landscape and of the countryside. Nowhere has this attitude been more apparent and effective than in the Forestry Commission, and this book provides valuable advice and support to this aim.

Dame Sylvia Crowe DBE PPILA

Introduction

Culture, symbolism and values

Patterns in the landscape

The importance of a visual vocabulary

The design process

How to use this book

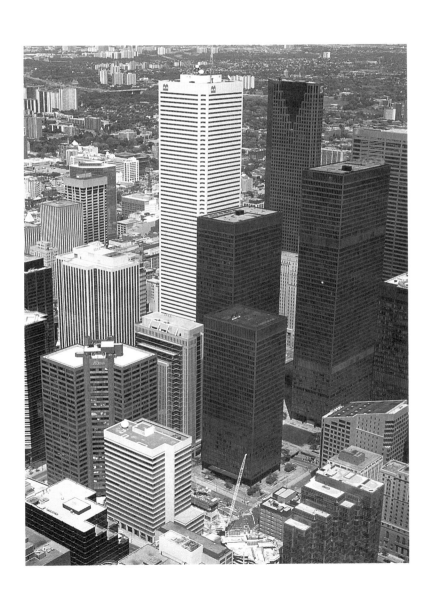

Introduction

From the moment we are born we gradually become aware of our surroundings. At first we can only focus on our mother's face and then we begin to see further away, to the room and to other members of the family. Our world is small and very limited. As older children we explore our neighbourhood or areas we visit on holiday. Later, as adults we may travel more extensively and gain knowledge of areas much wider afield.

Through this process of growing and developing, through learning and accepting or questioning what we are told we become partially shaped by our surroundings and our experiences. Eventually, each one of us, each of the five billion people on the earth has a unique view of the world. This view is full of likes and dislikes, detailed knowledge of some areas, ignorance of others and of course it is constantly changing. We hold both rational and irrational opinions and make huge assumptions based on this personal view.

Culture, symbolism and values

This personal view is contained within a cultural framework. Different societies, countries and cultures use and view the landscape in different ways and produce different land use patterns. The neat hedgerow-bordered fields and cosy villages which epitomize England in the minds of many people arose as a response to economic forces operating in a particular time, place and cultural context very different from those operating in the USA which have produced the high-rise, large-scale urban landscapes which epitomize that country. The landscapes of western, Christian cultures are varied but related to each other by certain sets of values and differ very markedly from those of Moslem, Hindu or Buddhist societies which each have their own deeply rooted cultural attitudes to the land.

Although we may not recognize it at first, there is also strong symbolism attached to particular aspects of the landscape. Some of it may relate back to our earliest origins as a species where the landscape was the habitat in which our ancestors lived and provided refuge and places of safety or views of land where game or enemies might be observed. Some symbols are concerned with secular or religious power and some are symbolic of the ideals or aspirations at different phases in the development of a particular society.

Compared with all the rest (so far as we know) of the animal kingdom, only humans perceive the world as a place full of meanings. Only we ascribe values to the environment about us. Insects and most lower animals probably only focus on the minute detail around them or sense generally hazy distinctions of more distant areas. Higher animals can identify nesting sites, recognize the same place year after year, select good hunting areas and so clearly must have some understanding of what they sense around them. We see our surroundings as an interrelated pattern of component parts arranged in certain ways. We attempt to make sense and order out of the apparent chaos.

The range of values we attach to the landscape varies with our closeness to or use of it. A farmer who derives his living from the land may view a pattern of fields and crops as a healthy and productive landscape where the soil is carefully nurtured to reach the full potential for food production. An ecologist concerned with the conservation of wildlife may look at the same landscape and consider it an impoverished habitat, sterile and devoid of most of its value through the very activities which give the farmer satisfaction. A city dweller unconnected with the land may see it as a place where he can get away from the pressures of urban life, understanding it in a superficial way and treating it as a backdrop or setting for his recreational activities.

Another of our concerns is the desire for stability and continuity in the ever changing world. If a place seems likely to stay the same we can usually be content with it, and through familiarity we can accept its shortcomings. Drastic change often brings anxiety, uncertainty and a loss of the sense of continuity and permanence which has been there (or so it seems) since childhood. This fear of change is often perceived to be worse than the actual circumstance of change itself.

One of the reasons for this is the lack of understanding of the processes at work in creating and altering a landscape over time. This is one more result of the superficial attitude of many people who see the landscape as a picture, a constant scene which can be preserved as it is indefinitely. This problem has been recognized by Sylvia Crowe in her book *A Pattern of Landscape*.

Patterns in the landscape

We must understand and recognize, therefore, that whatever our views, our cultural background or the values we attach to certain landscapes, we perceive them as patterns. As we grow we learn to recognize more and more of them. Instead of seeing these patterns as merely a picture, pretty or otherwise, it is vital that we understand their origins. Some may be the result of pure ecological processes interacting with landform and climate; others are the result of human activity interacting with natural processes yet not consciously planned or designed with any aesthetic objective in mind. Yet more are specifically designed to appeal to our aesthetic senses. None of these landscapes is static; all are subject to evolution and change over time as the result of natural or man-made processes. The pace of change will vary and some changes may be sudden and abrupt while others are more gradual.

If we can therefore identify the morphology of a landscape, put it into its cultural context and understand the processes which formed it we can use that information to inform decisions about its future use, conservation, development or management. We will be able to predict the patterns which will result from certain changes and judge them from an aesthetic point of view. In this way the processes at work in the landscape and the pressures and tendencies for change can be related to our responses and the values attached by our own society and culture.

The importance of a visual vocabulary

All this mix between ourselves, our idiosyncracies, personal preferences and anxieties makes the lot of anyone whose job it is to conserve, develop or manage the environment a very difficult one. Not only does a way have to be found to take account of all these views as well as the physical attributes of the world; there also has to be a recognition of personal views and the way these colour one's perception. Some things are fairly clear cut. There is often a great deal of consensus in the population about the best course of action to resolve a particular problem e.g. lead emission from car exhausts. However, when the subject turns away from the objectivity of science towards the perceived subjectivity of design and aesthetics then the job is far from easy. Resolving some problems may be simpler than others – product design for example, where if customers do not like a product they will not buy it and the 'market' will decide what is a good solution. In architecture the client or committee responsible for a building may be a limited number of people whose views are easy to reconcile. All of this becomes more difficult if the true and wider number of users' views are to be considered: for example, those of the general public.

In the wider landscape and especially public spaces or publicly accessible areas the owners or occupiers of these areas are not necessarily the sole 'users' if the large numbers who look at, use in various ways and care about what they see are taken into account. The actions of people which affect these landscapes – by planners, landscape architects, engineers, foresters and farmers for example – need to be exercised with a great deal of care. Increasingly the public care about the condition of the environment in all its forms and feel they have a right to a say in what happens in it. Given that this is so and that there are many people whose views need to be taken into account we need a way of understanding what we are looking at and of knowing how to use that understanding as a step in the design and management process.

It is at this point that we need to consider the place of aesthetics and the pursuit of beauty. As Nan Fairbrother pointed out in her book *The Nature Of Landscape Design*: 'Man is an animal who consciously creates landscape: the only species which deliberately alters the design of its environment for no other reason than to give itself aesthetic pleasure'. If we look back over the millennia since human culture first developed, for example, from Sumer in Mesopotamia onwards, we find that we have always taken delight in the appearance of things, from simply decorated early pottery to religious structures, palace complexes, gardens and hunting grounds. We certainly value some landscapes more than others on the grounds of their appearance, otherwise there would be no common consensus over which areas to protect for their scenic beauty, for example. It is perhaps a feature of western society in recent decades that appearances have been considered less important than function. The Modern Movement in architecture, for example, with its honesty of trying to express form out of function has not found a great deal of support among the users of many of the buildings it has produced. This may in part be due to the desire to be able to understand a building or urban landscape in terms of visual as well as functional patterns at a human scale, or it might be that many people consider them 'ugly'.

It is also worth recognizing that scenic or aesthetic values are a legitimate 'product' of the landscape: it is well known that people will pay more for a house with an attractive view than for one without, and that the economies of many areas rely heavily on tourism where visitors come to admire the scenery, or use a beautiful landscape as a setting for other forms of recreation.

One of the problems now facing designers is that the movement back towards a concern for human scale, for decoration and variety is often confused and expressed in superficial, naive terms easily turned by the unscrupulous into a cosmetic pastiche – reverting to the problem identified by Sylvia Crowe. Perhaps one of the reasons for this breakdown of understanding between designers and the public is the lack of a common language of visual expression enabling a proper debate on aesthetic issues as described above. What we require, therefore, is an aesthetic vocabulary which enables us not only to identify pattern but which allows us to say much more than 'I like that landscape' or 'I do not like that building'. In particular, we need a vocabulary which allows two or more people to discuss and evaluate what they see (or a proposed design) and to discuss its pros and cons in a rational and informed way so that a view on the value of a particular landscape or a proposed course of action which involves aesthetics can be reached which has a broad agreement.

This book presents just such a vocabulary. A key component is the use of certain definitions for particular terms with which nearly everyone can agree. The understanding, meanings and uses to which these particular terms can be put are demonstrated in abstract and real examples. These terms are 'visual design principles'. Many of them are already accepted or are long established, while some are more scientific or objective than others. What has been lacking in the past has been a clearly rational and structured way of presenting them which is accessible and easily understood by people who are not professional artists or designers. This was recognized by Duncan Campbell in 1975 and it is from the base provided by his attempts to develop a rational approach, developed later by Oliver Lucas and latterly by the author, that this book has evolved. Previous work has either tended to concentrate on a purely fine art approach or to have been more concerned with architecture. None has so far dealt in detail with the range from small-scale urban to large-scale wild landscapes.

The design process

How do we use this vocabulary? All too often design has been carried out in a linear, problem-solving fashion: survey, analysis, design, with the emergence of the result following a rational, deterministic route. This is exemplified in much of the work of the past few decades, especially in the approach used by McHarg. Creativity becomes stifled by the method in which form follows function and there is little room for either a conscious desire to achieve a beautiful result, or for sensitive emulation of natural processes in a directed way. Another shortcoming is the lack of a stage in which processes and appearances are matched and understood, and there is a tendency to rely on map-based assessments where the logic of the analytical process is paramount.

The first stage of the design process should be aimed at identifying the patterns found in the existing landscape using the vocabulary and expressing them in spatial terms, followed by an analysis of the source of the pattern and any processes at work. Following this the functional aspects related to the brief for the site can be added and inspiration sought for the direction of the design from the existing patterns, harnessing the processes or working with them. If the existing pattern is one which for some reason should not be perpetuated, then the aesthetic requirements may be obvious but a solution requires more creative, perhaps abstract thinking. This should result in a design in which function and aesthetics are fused instead of one being subservient to the other or considered mere decoration. The method should also allow for a critical assessment of the design where aesthetic criteria can be used alongside checklists of function or cost. Far from providing a strait-jacket it should free creative expression in an area where trade-offs between functional and aesthetic aspects are common and where all too often a reductionist approach to quality versus cost compromises the pursuit of excellence.

Design is of course about much more than composing elements into visually pleasing arrangements. It also involves balancing function and cost with aesthetics. Managers are mostly fluent in the first two aspects but less happy when dealing with aesthetics. I believe this is partly due to the mystique attached to design and its commonly perceived subjective nature. Once the rational basis of design is explained pragmatic people are usually more willing to treat the subject with the same seriousness they attach to practicalities and cost. I hope that this book will provide designers and non-designers alike with a common language of aesthetics so that better and more informed discussions about proposals for the future visual management of our environment can be made.

How to use this book

The presentation of the principles follows a three-tier structure. First all the basic elements from which all landscapes are composed are defined and discussed. Each of these basic elements may be varied in a number of ways. They may also be organized into different patterns. It is the combination of these three components which describes the patterns to be found in the existing landscape or produces visual designs or new patterns. A good design is one where the chosen variables and modes of organization are positive and harmonious. A bad design is where they are negative and disharmonious, irrespective of personal taste or preference.

Basic elements

Point, line, plane, solid volume, open volume.

Variables

Number, position, direction, orientation, size, shape (form), interval, texture, density, colour, time, light, visual force, visual inertia.

Organization

Objectives: diversity, unity, *genius loci*.

Spatial cues: nearness, closure, interlock, continuity, similarity, figure and ground.

Structural elements: balance, tension, rhythm, proportion, scale.

Ordering: axis, symmetry, hierarchy, datum, transformation.

Each section is structured as above. There is a logical order in the way each principle is treated but no reason why the book cannot be used as a reference manual. Cross-referencing helps the reader to understand the links between principles, and the summary points at the beginning of each section should provide a useful *aide-mémoire* of each topic. The illustrations are intended to clarify the points made. The case studies are used to demonstrate the application and interaction of several points at once.

1
Basic Elements

Point

Line

Plane

Volume

Combinations of elements

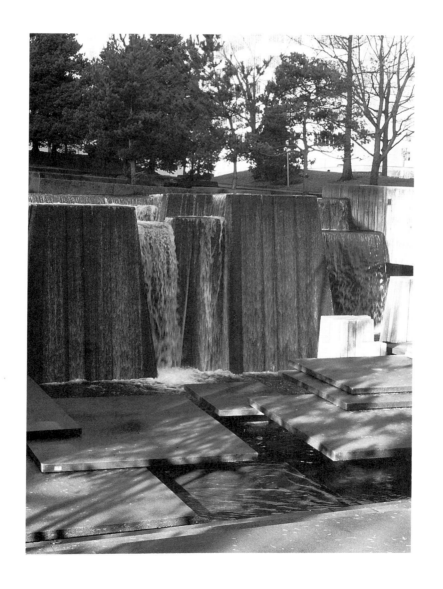

1

Basic Elements

Our environment of hills, water, woods, vegetation, buildings and artefacts provides a myriad of different landscape patterns which we see. To aid the understanding of their visual qualities, landscapes can be analysed in a fundamental and rational manner. The patterns we see are formed from the arrangements of different components. Every article or object that makes up one of these components can be regarded as a 'basic building block'.

Depending on how we see these objects – our distance from them, for example – we can treat them as one of four *basic elements* – a point, a line, a plane or a volume. We need to understand the attributes of each element before we see how they interact and the effects different variables and methods of organization have on the patterns so produced.

Point

- A point marks a position in space.
- Small objects can be seen as points.
- Point features can be associated with assertions of power or ownership and can be symbolic in all kinds of ways.

A point, strictly speaking, has no dimension but marks a position in space. Initially, therefore, it can be indicated by some secondary means such as crossed or focusing lines or a point of light. In reality, a point needs some dimension to attract the attention and in the landscape small or distant objects may be regarded as points. A bale of straw, a lone tree, a small distant building are common examples.

Quite often in the past points have been defined with a particular purpose such as to mark out territory, to assert ownership or dominion over an area, to act as landmarks, to

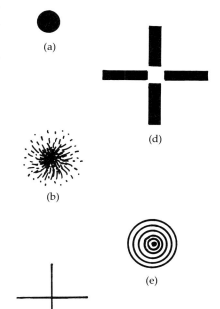

(a) A point.
(b) A point of density.
(c) Crossed lines mark a point . . .
(d) . . . as do focused lines . . .
(e) . . . or concentric circles emphasizing a centre.

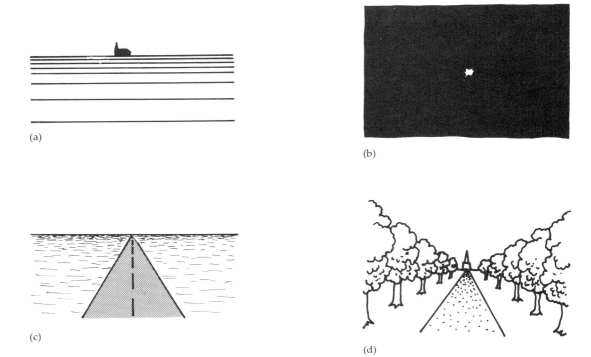

Many features in the landscape can be regarded as points:
    (a) a church or similar object on the horizon;
    (b) a point of light such as a star in the sky;
    (c) the point where parallel lines appear to converge;
    (d) lines and a feature on the horizon create a focal point.

A single tree acts as a point in this otherwise featureless prairie landscape.

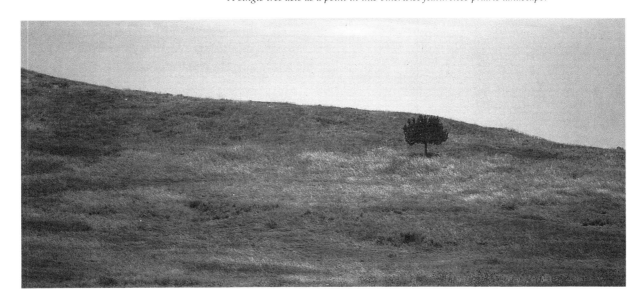

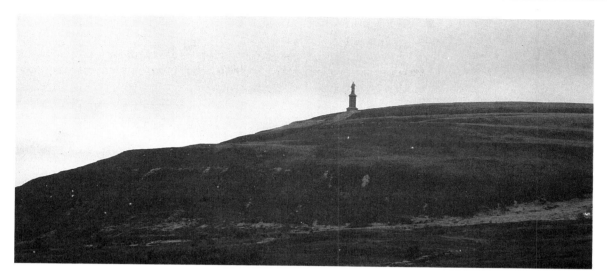

This memorial high on a hillside in Sutherland is a point which catches the eye from many directions. This prominence ensures that the person or persons whom the monument commemorates will never be entirely forgotten.

provide a focus for a grand design, or merely to provide an interest in a featureless landscape. Examples include early megalithic standing stones or Bronze Age barrows on the skyline which may have established ownership over the nearby land; the lone church spire; the obelisk at the end of a grand avenue; a war memorial or a monument to a person or event. All these say something about the society and the position within it of the people who put them there.

Line

- Extending a point in one dimension creates a line.
- Lines can be implied by the location of points.
- Lines can be imaginary yet still exert influence.
- Edges of planes can be seen as lines.
- Lines can have their own properties.
- Natural lines are common and important in the landscape.
- Man-made lines are also numerous.
- Lines as boundaries are used extensively.
- Lines can act as defining elements in architecture.

While a point is, strictly speaking, non-dimensional, a line is an extension of a point in one dimension. It needs thickness to register and can have specific properties in the way it is drawn or created: for example clean, fuzzy, irregular or discontinuous. The edge or edges of planes are also lines at certain distances as are the boundaries between different colours and textures. A line can be implied by the position of points or the association of edges. It can also have a distinct shape and with that imply a direction and force or energy.

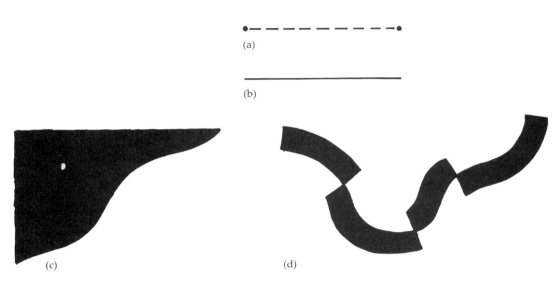

(a)

(b)

(c)

(d)

(a) A line is formed by extending a point in one dimension.
(b) A simple line thus formed.
(c) The boundary between two shapes or planes is a line.
(d) The edges of planes laid end to end can create a continuous line as the eye runs along the contiguous edge.

(a)

(b)

(c)

(d)

Lines can have different qualities:
  (a) a broken line;
  (b) a line of variable width;
  (c) a fuzzy or indistinct line;
  (d) a clear, simple line.

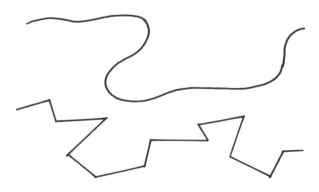

Lines can have different characters:
  (a) a smooth flowing line;
  (b) a jagged, stiff line.

In the landscape, lines are very numerous and important. As natural lines they exist in stream patterns, tree trunks, edges of vegetation patterns, the sky line or horizon, and rock strata. Field boundaries, roads and plough furrows are examples of man-made lines.

Perhaps it is as boundaries delineating ownership, land use or territory that lines have meant most over the ages. Lines set out during the enclosure of common land in Britain, the land grants of colonial territories or the international boundaries which divide cultures have helped to determine patterns which have had very long-term effects on the landscapes of whole countries. Lines of communication – canals, railways, roads – also establish their own patterns. Sometimes these different lines are in harmony; sometimes they cut across each other to create discordance and conflict.

In the built environment, lines can be important as defining or controlling elements in architecture or urban planning: the building line along which the frontages of buildings are set, sight lines or roof lines are examples of these.

Imaginary lines such as contour lines linking points of common elevation can have an effect. For instance the tree line in mountainous country (a combination of elevation and climate), the constraints placed on road gradients, or the creation of level construction or cultivation terraces can all be determined by their relation to contour levels.

One of the strongest lines is the horizon: the boundary between land or sea and sky. Here this line is emphasized by the simple, horizontal surface of the land. It allows the observer to concentrate on the cloud formations flowing across the landscape. Caithness, Scotland.

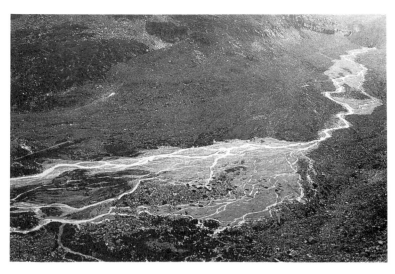

An intertwining network of lines created by moving stream beds as meltwater escaping from a glacier slows down and deposits its load of sediment. Hohe Tauern National Park, Austria.

Stone walls create a strongly defined pattern of lines across the landscape. Here in the Yorkshire Dales in England the light picks up the pattern where it resembles a net draped over the hillside.

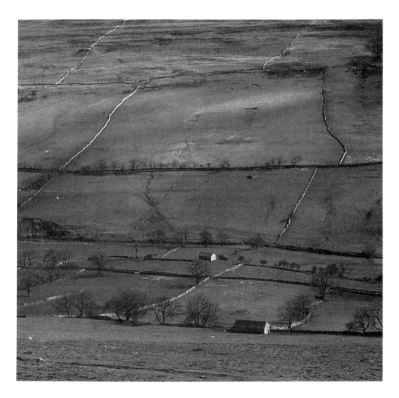

Plane

- A one-dimensional line is extended to produce a two-dimensional plane.
- Planes can be flat, curved or twisted.
- Planes can be implied as well as real.
- Planes in different positions may enclose space.
- Naturally perfect planes are few.
- The land surface is a plane.
- Faces of built forms are planes.
- Planes can be used as media for other treatment.
- Planes can be used for their inherent qualities such as reflection.

By extending the one-dimensional line into two dimensions we can form a plane. Of itself it has no depth or thickness, only length and width. A piece of paper or a thin wall can be regarded as more or less pure planes for all practical purposes. Often the surface of a three-dimensional object seen close to is perceived as a plane. Planes can be simple, flat, curved or twisted. They need not be continuous nor need they be real – they may be implied as in the 'picture plane'. Where planes enclose space they may assume a specific function such as floor, wall or roof planes.

In the natural world, there are few 'perfect' planes. Regular, symmetrical crystalline surfaces are quite rare. The undisturbed, calm surface of a pool or lake is a near-perfect plane and is consciously used in design for this property allied to the reflective qualities also present in the still water surface.

Other planes include the surface of the land. This may act as a floor plane for some other structure. A closely spaced row of trees can form a vertical plane while overhanging branches can form a roof plane. A space-frame or pergola may also define more transparent planes. These begin to enclose space and so create an open volume.

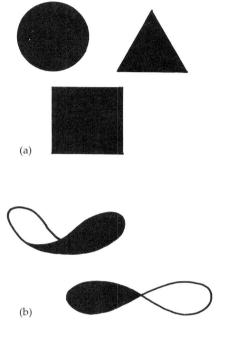

(a)

(b)

(a) Flat, simple, geometric planes;
(b) curved and twisted planes.

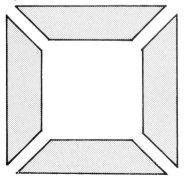

Planes may perform a function, especially in a built environment.

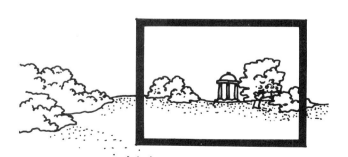

The picture plane: the implied surface which forms the interface between reality and the image in a painting or photograph.

19

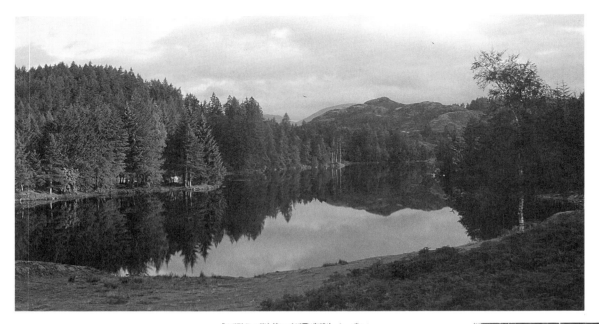

Completely still water is a perfect plane. Here at Tarn Hows in the English Lake District the perfect reflection and the deep shadows allow the water surface to contrast perfectly with the natural shapes around it. (Courtesy Oliver Lucas)

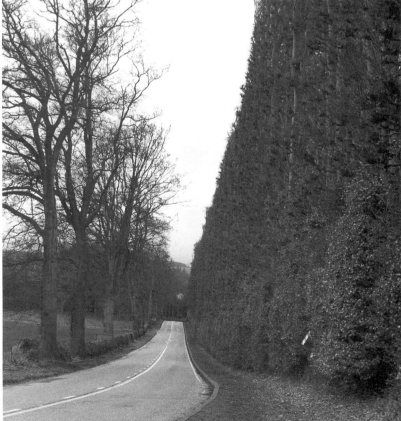

An interesting vertical plane formed from the closely spaced trees which have been clipped to produce the 'Hundred-foot-high hedge' at Meiklour, Perthshire, Scotland.

In design terms the plane is best understood as the medium for other treatment such as the application of texture or colour or as a device to enclose space. Many of the variables we shall examine in the next chapter rely on the plane to provide a base medium. The plane can however be used in its own right: the reflecting pool is one classic example. The fields used for many games – football, cricket, bowls or tennis – depend on precisely laid out plane surfaces. Some buildings feature horizontal planes to achieve specific effects such as the emphasis of the ground plane with a parallel, flat roof. The vertical planes forming the sheer glass façades on some skyscrapers may produce reflections of the sky or surrounding buildings.

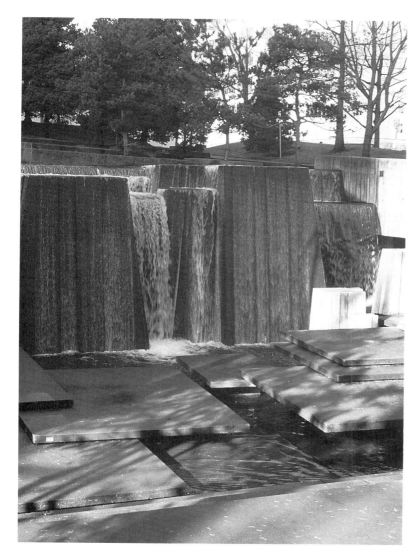

A superb abstract composition of planes used in a fountain by Laurence Halprin in Portland, Oregon. The overlapping horizontal planes (stable, still, dry) contrast with the vertical planes (unstable, running, wet) to form a harmonious, balanced composition.

Volume

- Volume is the three-dimensional extension of a two-dimensional plane.
- Volume can be solid or open.
- Solid volumes can be geometric or irregular.
- Buildings, landforms, trees and woods are all solid volumes – mass in space.
- Open volumes are defined by planes or other solid volumes – enclosed space.
- Interiors of buildings, deep valleys and the space beneath the forest canopy are all open volumes.

From two dimensions we move to three and so gain volume. There are two types of volume:

Solid volume – where the three-dimensional element forms a volume or mass in space.

Open volume – where a volume of space is enclosed by other elements such as planes.

Solid volumes can be geometric. Euclidean solids such as the cube, tetrahedron, sphere and cone are examples of this. In the landscape the Egyptian pyramids and other ancient man-made structures rank alongside more recent examples of geodesic spheres and glass cubes as examples of geometric volumes.

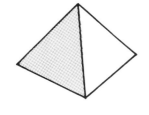
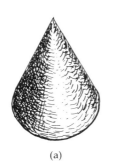
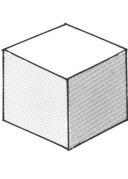
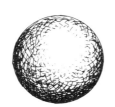
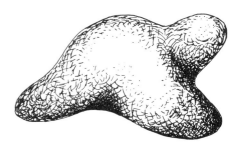
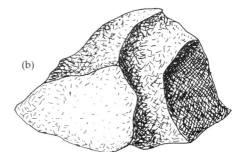

(a)

(b)

(a) Geometric solid volumes: typical Euclidean forms;
(b) irregular solid volumes: soft and rounded, hard and angular.

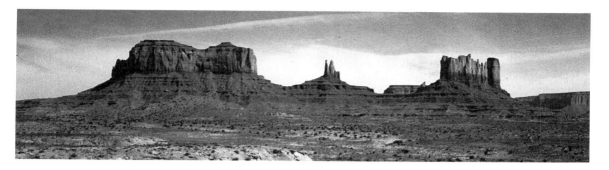

Natural solid volumes dominating the scene with their strong forms emphasized by the light and shade. Monument Valley, Utah, USA. (Courtesy Maggie Gilvray)

Irregular solid volumes are common. Some can be rounded and soft while others are angular and hard. Some of the most striking landforms are dominant volumes rising from planes. Ayers Rock in Australia and Devil's Tower in Wyoming are two evocative examples (see *Genius loci*). It is not surprising that such features carry spiritual values for the native people of both areas. Clean volcanic cones are other volumes of a semi-geometric form which can change and grow over time. Sand dunes change their shape with the wind and some move at a steady pace across the desert plains (see Direction).

A modern example of a geometric solid volume: a spherical building (actually composed of many small planes) at Expo '86, Vancouver, British Columbia.

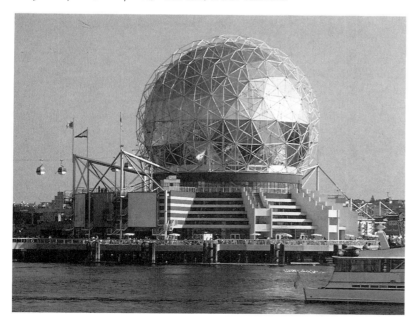

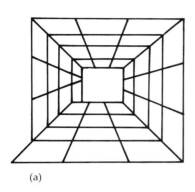

(a)

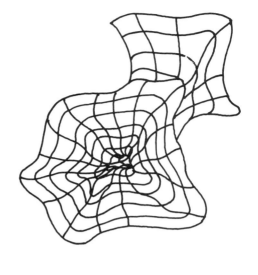

(b)

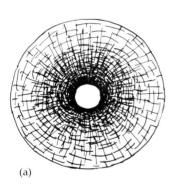

(a)

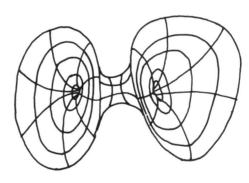

(a) Regular and (b) irregular open volumes

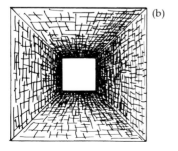

(b)

Tunnels, tubes or pipes: these open volumes are framed by enclosing planes.

Single buildings or groups of buildings which do not enclose space are solid volumes when viewed from outside. Some large ones such as power stations dominate the flat landscapes around them.

Not all volumes seem heavy or truly solid – clouds floating across the sky or trees and woods when leafless are light or transparent masses.

Open volumes may be defined by an open spatial structure such as a lattice or they may be more definite, bounded by solid planes to form a hollow or void. More ambiguous, perhaps, are steel and glass transparent buildings such as glasshouses at botanic gardens which enclose a separate climate and blur the distinction between enclosed and open space.

Out in the landscape the main enclosing elements may be solid volumes such as landforms creating an open volume in a narrow, deep valley. Trees and woods can contain spaces and create open volumes between them – as in a designed parkland landscape – or inside them as in the case of a small ride or small open space or felled area. Beneath the forest canopy the overhead branches, the ground and the implied planes of the tree trunks can also create a volume.

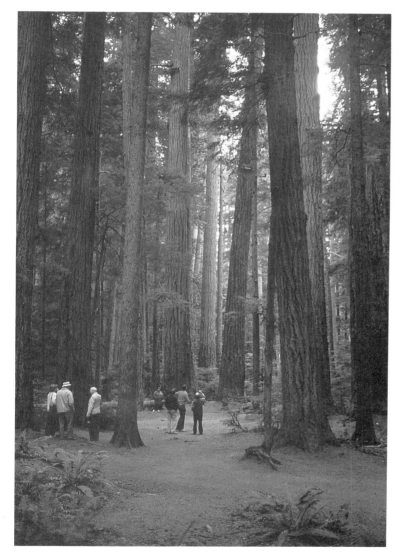

Beneath the forest canopy, enclosed by the tree crowns overhead, the ground plane and the tree trunks, a spacious open volume is created. It is all the more dramatic here because of the large size of the trees and the open character of the vegetation. Cathedral Grove, Vancouver Island, British Columbia.

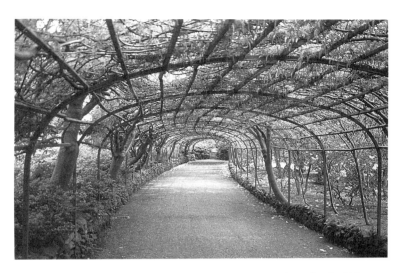

A sinuous open volume created by a pergola and covered in a dense thatch of laburnum: a recreation of the woodland canopy tamed by man. Bodnant Gardens, Gwynedd, Wales.

A large open volume formed by the enclosing façades (planes) of the buildings and the pavement ground plane: a well-defined space, formal in character. Piazza San Marco, Venice, Italy.

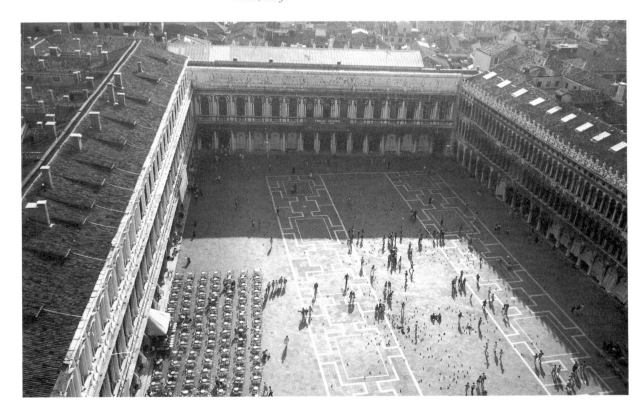

Some of the most impressive urban spaces are the result of careful positioning of planes (building façades) to create open volumes. These may interconnect and flow from one to another in a carefully planned fashion.

Combinations of elements

- It is rare for one basic element to exist in isolation.
- Distinctions between elements may be blurred.
- Distance may change the perception of which element is present.

It is rare for one element to exist in isolation. Normally they are found in combination. Moreover, it is possible for the distinctions between them to be quite blurred and ambiguous. A number of points may appear as a line or a plane while at different distances planes may be seen as points or lines (edges) and faces of solid or

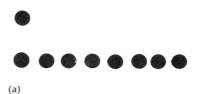

(a)

  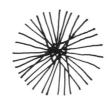

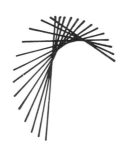

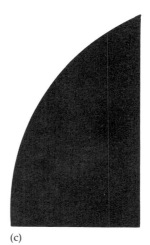

(c)

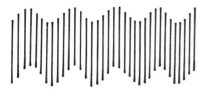

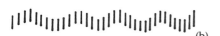

(b)

Some examples of the interchangeability of elements in combination.
(a) A single point when multiplied can become a line . . .
(b) . . . or a plane . . .
. . . as can a number of lines, either flat or curved.
(c) The edge of a plane is a line . . .

Combinations of elements

(d) . . . while a number of planes can be a line . . .
(e) . . . or enclose a volume.

(d)

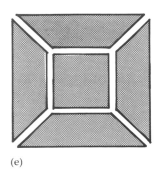

(e)

In this precisely engineered weir the perfectly horizontal plane of the water held behind it drops over the edge. The resulting sweeping, smoothly curved line contrasts sharply with the jagged rocks below, providing further contrast of stillness and movement, quietness and noise.

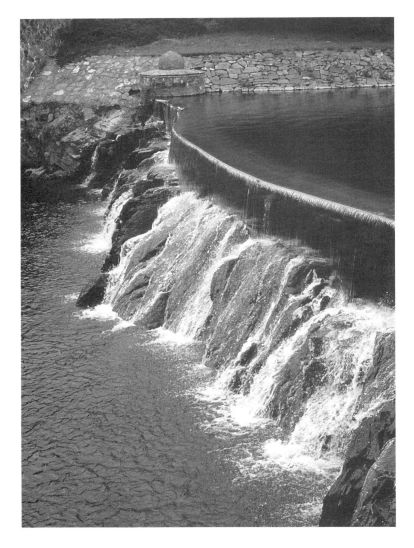

open volumes. This changeability provides stimulation as we behold a scene or composition. This shift as we move from one scale to another has important connotations for our ability to understand patterns over different distances or from shifting observer positions (see Scale).

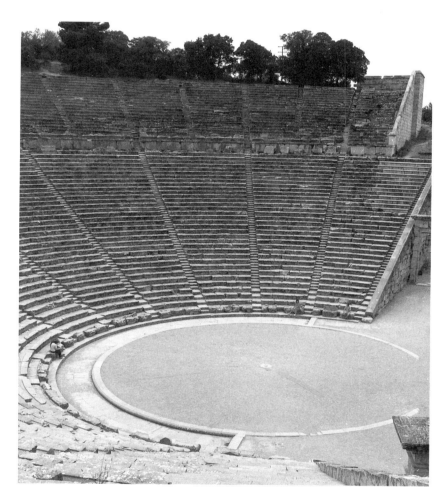

These terraces are laid out on a curving plane in the form of an inverted, truncated cone in the ancient Greek theatre at Epidaurus. The result is visually harmonious – plane, horizontal and vertical lines focusing on the central circular plane, the orchestra. It is also perfect for views down to the actors and also for acoustics – people seated on the topmost terrace can hear a pin drop in the centre of the orchestra.

2
Variables

Number

Position

Direction

Orientation

Size

Shape (form)

Interval

Texture

Density

Colour

Time

Light

Visual force

Visual inertia

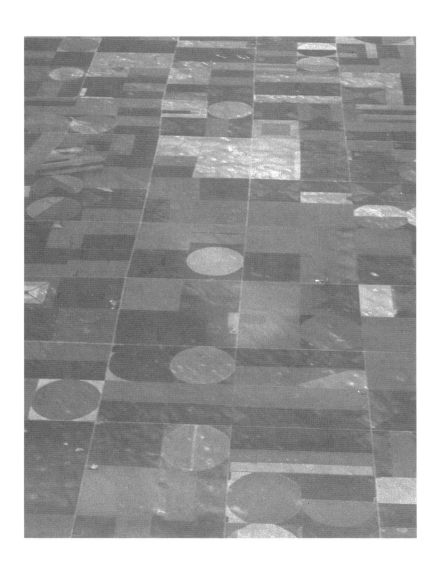

2

Variables

In summary, point, line, plane and volume are the basic mass-space elements of visual expression. Every form of life that we see or visualize can be simplified to one of these elements or some combination of them.

GARRETT, 1969

The basic elements can be seen in relation to light, colour, time and movement. We see them in many different ways. There are, however, a limited but fundamental number of ways of varying them.

Number, position, direction, orientation;
size, shape (form), interval, texture, density, colour;
time, light, visual force, visual inertia.

In this chapter we are going to examine each of these variables in turn in the context of the basic elements described in Chapter 1. At this stage we are not yet concerned with the organization of elements into patterns; yet without a clear understanding of the effects of the variables the final patterns will not make sense. In many ways it is the interaction of the variables with the organizing principles which determines whether the overall visual effect is harmonious or not. It is also logical to proceed from the simple breakdown of components into basic elements to the next level of sophistication: the variables.

Number

• Elements exist in isolation or as one of a number.
• Greater numbers usually mean more complexity.

(a)

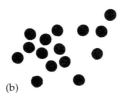

(b)

(a) One element.
(b) A number of elements: a pattern
starts to form and interaction occur.

- Number is expressed in different ways.
- Ambiguity may exist in what comprises number.
- Ratios and series of numbers can be found.

Single elements may exist by themselves with apparently little reference to their surroundings. By being repeated, added to or otherwise multiplied each element will exist in visual relationship to another and certain spatial effects come into play. Generally, the more there is of an element, the more complex the pattern or design.

Exactly how a number of elements is expressed can vary. A single complete form can be repeated to form a pattern. Conversely a single form may itself be composed of a series of others. The segments or portions of the original form may be redistributed to create another form or pattern. At different scales what appear to be single elements may be seen as parts of a greater whole or may themselves be composed of a number of elements not recognizable at a distance.

Some aspects of number may be ambiguous. A row of terraced houses comprising a number of units will appear as a single form. A clump of trees growing closely together may develop the shape and size of a single tree of the same age.

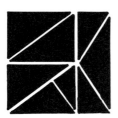

An element of one shape composed of a
number of elements of different shape.

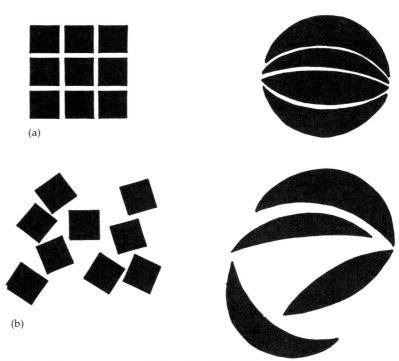

(a)

(b)

(a) A single form may be composed of a number of elements . . .
(b) . . . or be divided into a number of segments or parts.

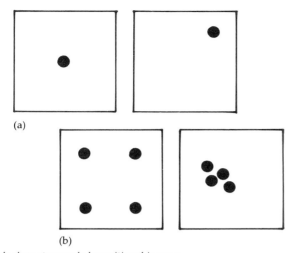

(a)

(b)

(a) A single element can only be positioned in space.
(b) A number of elements are positioned both in space and in relation to each other.

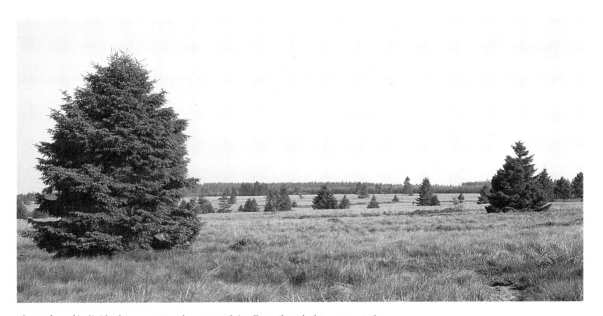

A number of individual trees scattered across a plain. Even though they appear to be randomly distributed a pattern begins to emerge, the more complex as the number increases and more variable with size differences. Each tree is seen in conjunction with its neighbours. Ardennes, Belgium.

Number may also involve certain ratios or series. Some of these, odd numbers for example, may lead to elements being placed in a certain arrangement such as the quincunx (an arrangement of five elements into a cross shape). Other number series may be used to create asymmetrical designs (l, 3, 5, 7, 9 . . . etc.) while some have been used as the bases of abstract

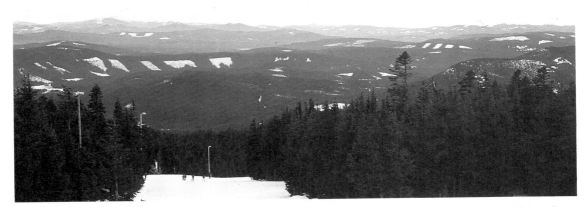

A large number of clear cuts in the Mount Hood National Forest in Oregon, USA can be seen from this viewpoint. As more are added the increasing number starts to dominate and the cumulative effect has an enormous visual impact which a smaller number would not have.

A group of cabins in a forest. The position of each depends on many factors: whether to give each of them a good view, how to arrange the access and services, whether to orientate them in an architectural relationship or to relate them to the landform.

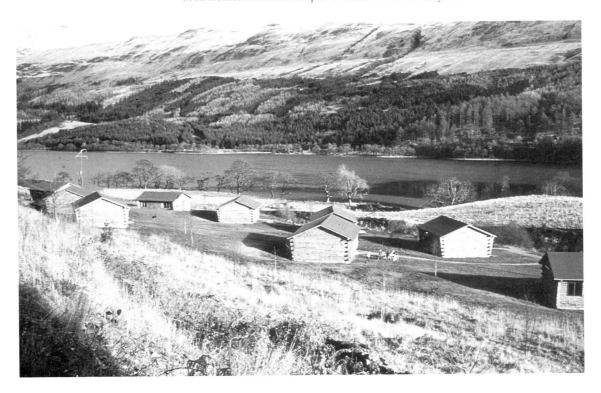

mathematical systems of proportion (such as the Fibonacci series in which the last two numbers are added to arrive at the next). (See Proportion.)

The effect of increasing number may result in practical complications when resolving a design. Siting a single building in the landscape is a simpler task than that of siting two or more: the visual relationships of a complex of buildings, views to and from them, access and service provision are generally more complicated to design.

Position

- There are three primary positions – horizontal, diagonal, vertical.
- Points are positioned with respect to the space.
- Lines cause visual forces and tensions depending on how they are positioned.
- Planes may begin to interlock or overlap.
- The position of elements may interact with landform.
- Building positions can be related to each other or to the landform or to other features.
- Non-visual reasons for position still influence visual pattern and structure.

Forms in space can occupy three primary positions:
Horizontal – parallel to the horizon
Vertical – perpendicular to the horizon and man's upright position
Diagonal – between the two, oblique.

These three positions can have quite powerful connotations. Horizontal forms seem to be stable, at rest, inert and ground-hugging. Vertical forms have long been used to make a statement or assert a relationship with the heavens. The vertical position also represents growth: for example tree trunks, plant stems. Diagonal positions create more dynamic effects and may appear unstable.

Elements can be related to each other through their position – parallel, end-to-end, crossed.

Points can be positioned at the centre of a space, outside it, towards the side or touching the edge. Each of these sets up a relationship which may invoke a sense of stability and balance or force, movement and tension. In each case it is the relationship of the element to the total space which creates the effect (see Visual force, Balance).

Lines with their strong single dimension also start to cause visual forces and tensions depending on their relative positions.

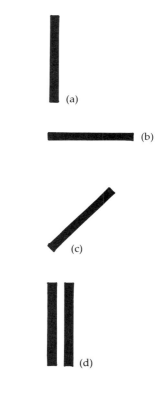

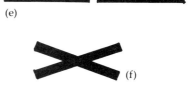

Some basic positions:
(a) Vertical – perpendicular to the horizon;
(b) Horizontal – parallel with the horizon;
(c) Diagonal – between (a) and (b) unstable;
and identical elements in relation to one another:
(d) parallel;
(e) end-to-end;
(f) crossed.

37

Position

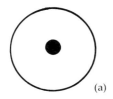

(a)

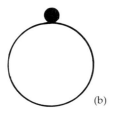

(b)

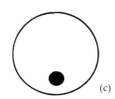

(c)

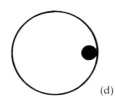

(d)

The implications of the relative positions of a point and a plane:
(a) inside, centred, stable;
(b) outside, centred, potentially unstable;
(c) inside, off centre, stable;
(d) inside, against the edge, dynamic.

A pair of crossed lines may produce different effects in relation to a space depending on their direction and whether they meet, extend beyond or stay inside the space. Different positions can strengthen or weaken the visual forces around the elements (see Visual force, Tension).

Planes can be positioned to follow the main axes of parallel with, diagonal to or at right angles to one another. The latter two positions can start to interlock or overlap with each other (see Spatial cues).

In the landscape the position of elements in relation to landform can produce very marked effects, particularly on the summits of hills. This is in part due to the visual forces in landform and also because the eye is attracted to hilltops. A line of electricity pylons crossing the skyline on a hill instead of in a valley produces visual tension as well as conflicting with visual forces. A sculpture or monument, on the other hand, may produce tension if it is not precisely on the summit.

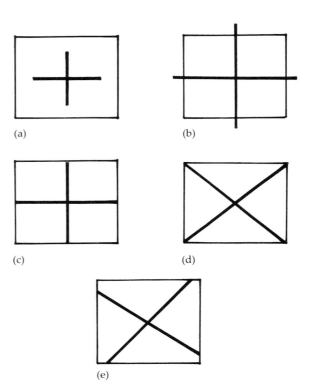

Some positions of crossed lines in relation to a plane:
(a) parallel and inside the edge – stable but floating;
(b) parallel and extending beyond the edge – stable and unified;
(c) parallel and touching the edge – subdividing the plane;
(d) diagonal, meeting at the corners – stable;
(e) diagonal but not quite meeting at the corners – unstable, creating tension.

(a)

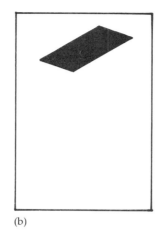

(b)

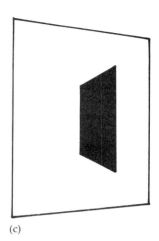

(c)

Two planes in relation to one another:
(a) parallel – stable, balanced though top heavy;
(b) diagonal – unstable, dynamic;
(c) perpendicular – stable, balanced.

The position of a building in the landscape needs to take account of the composition of volumes, planes and lines in order to maintain a harmonious balance (see Symmetry, Balance, Axis). Several buildings can be positioned to follow their inherent geometry (for instance grouped at right angles to one another), landform (such as being aligned parallel to the contours), or other features such as the edge of a space defined by trees or woodland.

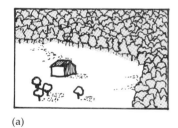

(a)

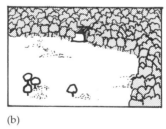

(b)

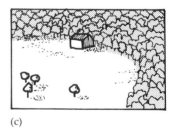

(c)

Options for the position of a building in the landscape.
(a) A small building positioned in an open space away from a woodland edge. The building (a point or small volume) takes over the space visually but does not interrupt the line of the woodland edge. Functionally, the building receives a lot of sunlight but there will be other visual effects not shown, such as access routes or car parking, which may reduce the simplicity of the design. The building does not appear to be tied down in the landscape.
(b) This option shows the building tucked into the woodland edge where it is fairly well hidden. The open space is not intruded into and all additional functional requirements can be hidden away. The building will, however, receive little light and the roof and gutters may collect leaves in the autumn.
(c) Here the building is aligned with the woodland edge which helps draw the eye to it creating a focal composition. There is good light, aspect and access; parking can be hidden among the trees. The position against the line helps to tie it into the landscape and it does not occupy as much space as (a).

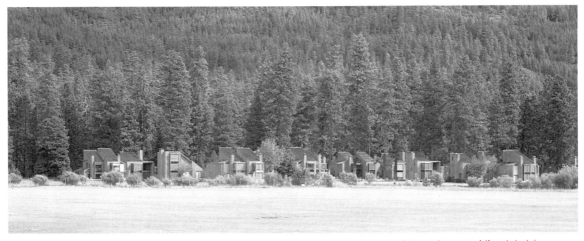

Small buildings positioned to maximize views, sunshine and access while minimizing physical and visual intrusion on to the grassy plane of the golf course in the foreground. The wooded backdrop also helps to contain the buildings and screens access and parking. Black Butte Ranch, Oregon, USA.

The defensive line of Hadrian's Wall in Northumberland follows the edge of the Great Whin Sill. The position provides maximum natural advantage to the defenders who have good visibility over enemy territory and effective natural protection from attack. Visually, there is an extremely close relationship between the wall and the landform.

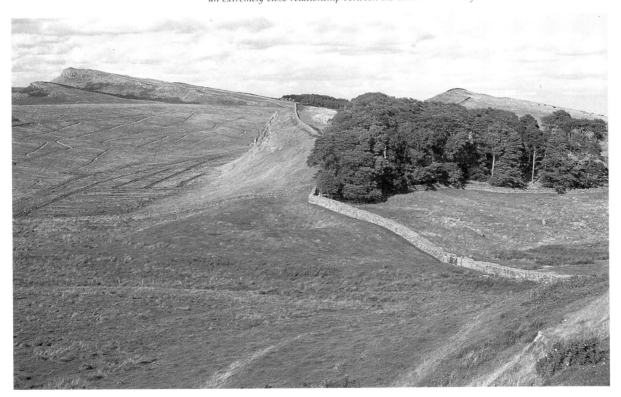

The position of forms may be determined by reasons other than the aesthetic, but which nevertheless produce strong visual images or effects. Sometimes religious activities involve placing forms in precise ways, such as at Stonehenge on Salisbury Plain or Inca mountaintop shrines in the Andes (see Orientation). Fortification and protection have also determined position – Iron Age hill forts on prominent hill tops, Hadrian's Wall on the whin sill in Northumberland, Krak des Chevaliers atop a rugged hill in Syria. Commerce and transport routes and their defence continue to be important in determining settlement position: for example river crossings such as Stirling on the Forth, Quebec on the St Lawrence, and Chicago located between two great lakes on the railway network. All of these examples have influenced the

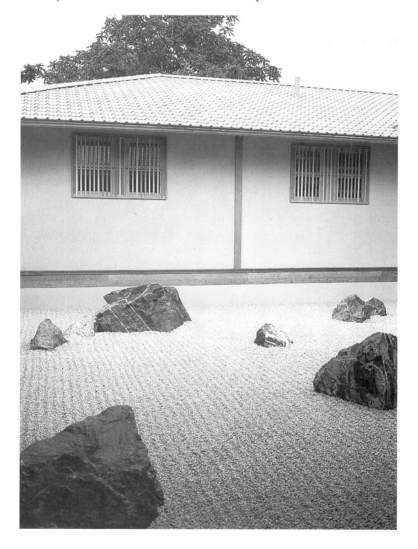

A Japanese Zen garden where the full effect is achieved by very precise positioning of the carefully selected stones in the raked ground. The combination of sizes, shapes and groupings is particularly important for achieving a harmonious balance. The designer will spend a long time deciding on the optimum position of each rock relative to the others.

pattern and structure of the landscape which is as visually expressive as it is historical, symbolic or functional.

In artistic terms the Zen garden from Japan where stones represent islands in a raked gravel sea relies on position in its most precise sense, since there is a great deal of care required to produce the near-perfect effect of the whole composition. Further symbolism exists here in terms of life and death or thoughts (the mind) in a void.

Direction

- Elements may be positioned according to a certain direction.
- The shape of an element may imply direction.
- Lines in the landscape may produce a sense of direction and invite the observer into the composition.
- Natural elements show direction according to forces such as wind and waves.

The position of an element may be determined according to a particular direction. Furthermore, it may not appear stable; it may imply movement, which is almost always thought of in terms of direction – for example up and down (vertical) or side to side (horizontal). The shape of the element may also reinforce the sense of direction; this is especially true of lines or linear shapes.

In the landscape, lines such as paths or roads often produce a sense of direction and lead the viewer towards them. This is particularly the case with curving lines which disappear tantalizingly around a corner. The position of clumps of trees may be precisely designed to direct the eye towards a particular feature.

Natural elements may display direction because of the way they have been formed or grown. Trees naturally grow towards a source of light or can be sculpted by the wind. Sand dunes all face the same way and move in the direction of the wind – this is reflected in their shape. Ripple marks on the sea shore left by the retreating tide reflect the movement of the waves (see Rhythm).

Perhaps the most dramatic manifestation of direction can be seen in the trees blown flat during the eruption of Mount St Helens in Washington, USA in 1980. They are all aligned in the same way in the direction of the blast, marking the path of the exploding mountain.

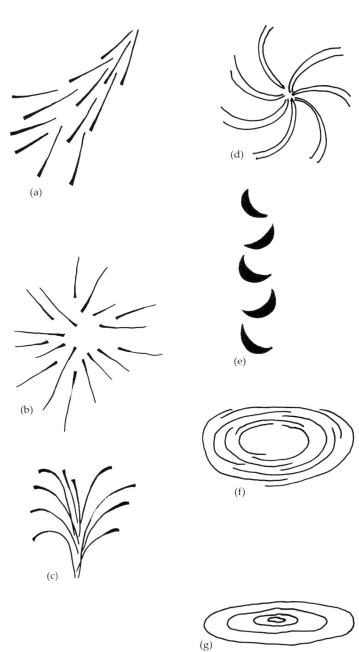

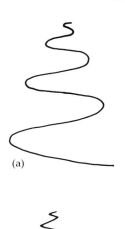

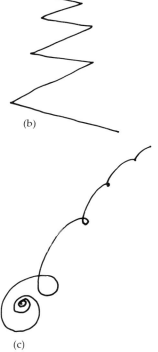

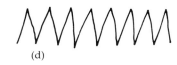

There are a number of different directions which can be expressed by elements:
(a) up and across – bottom left to top right;
(b) outwards;
(c) in and downwards;
(d) round and out;
(e) falling downwards, from side to side;
(f) round and round a central point;
(g) outwards from a centre.

The directional movement may have different qualities:
(a) winding smoothly ahead;
(b) ahead jerkily;
(c) out and up in a series of leaps;
(d) up and down quickly.

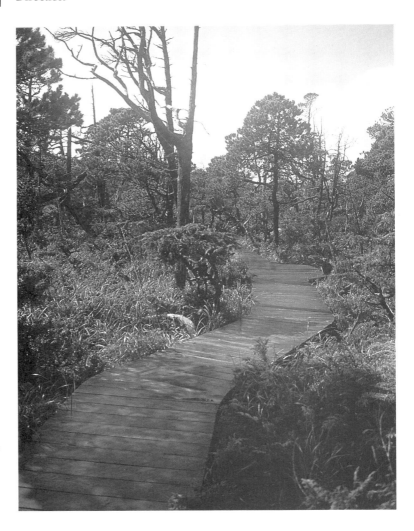

This boardwalk following a curved alignment leads the eye into the picture and makes us want to follow its direction in order to see what lies beyond. Shorepine Trail, Pacific Rim National Park, Vancouver Island, British Columbia.

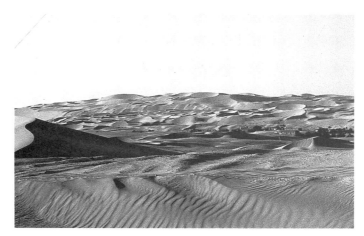

Sand dunes in the Arabian Desert. Their shape shows a strong pattern due to the direction of the prevailing wind constantly blowing the sand from left to right across the picture. United Arab Emirates. (Courtesy of Robert Bryant.)

44

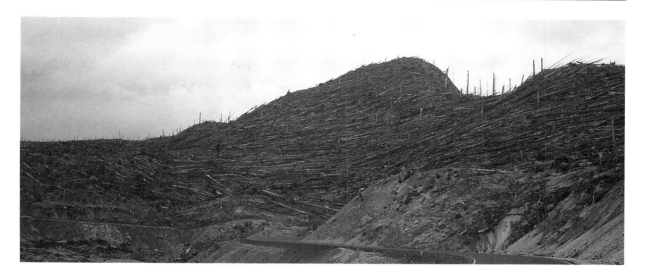

Orientation

- Orientation is a combination of position and direction.
- Orientation literally means 'facing east'.
- There are three types of orientation:

    according to compass direction;
    relative to ground plane;
    relative to viewer.

- Disorientation may be the aim of a design and carry symbolism with it.

Orientation is a combination of position and specific direction. Literally this means 'facing east' and refers to the compass direction towards which churches and mosques are invariably aligned.

Basically there are three types of orientation:
- according to the compass direction – not just towards the east but other points, for example, sunshine direction and angles, prevailing winds, sun and moon rise at certain times of the year;
- relative to another element, particularly the ground plane – level, tilted;
- relative to the viewer – the axis of a park as seen from the terrace of a great house, the angle of approach to a fortress as seen by a potential attacker.

A design may be intended to disorientate or confuse the viewer, as in a maze, or make a place appear bigger than it really is by twisting and turning paths.

The dramatic effect of the eruption of the volcano Mount St Helens in 1980 can be seen in these trees which were blown flat by the force of the blast. They are all aligned in the direction of the explosion, creating a vivid impression of its speed and strength. Washington, USA.

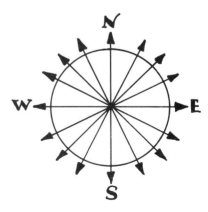

One major way of orienting elements is according to the points of the compass.

45

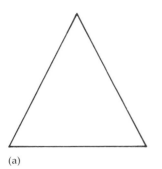
(a)

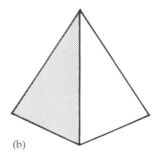
(b)

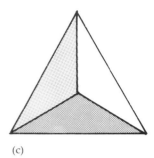
(c)

Here a form is oriented in relation to the observer:
(a) face on;
(b) edge on;
(c) tilted away.

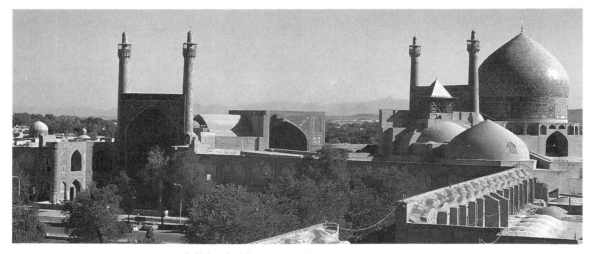

Religious buildings are usually oriented in a particular way. Here the Blue Mosque in Istanbul, Turkey, is oriented so that worshippers face Mecca. (Courtesy of Maggie Gilvray.)

This recumbent stone circle (dated to the late third millenium BC) is oriented in such a way that the moon rise and set, seen from a point within the circle, intersects the large horizontal stone thus being used to mark seasons or in religious rites associated with seasonal changes. Loanhead of Daviot, Aberdeenshire, Scotland.

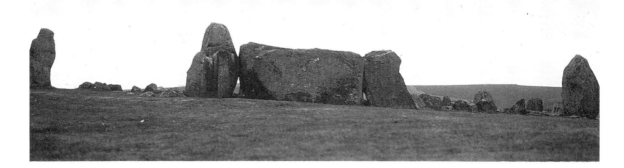

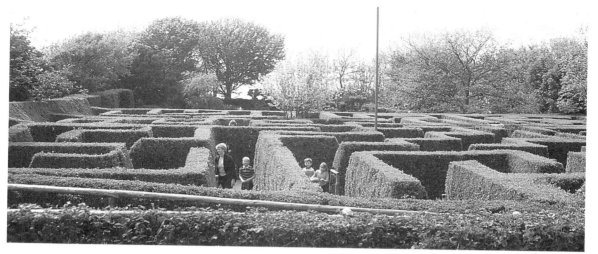

Size

- Size concerns the dimensions of elements.
- Extremes include tall/short, big/small, wide/narrow, shallow/deep.
- Size depends for its definition on a system of measurements which may be derived from many sources.
- Large, tall or deep forms are impressive and have been used to exert power.
- Smaller forms may be valued for their low impact.
- Plants and animals are limited in size owing to genetic and environmental factors.

Size concerns the dimensions of elements or parts of elements. Common size variations include tall/short, wide/narrow, large/small, shallow/deep.

A maze is designed to disorientate people. The hedges are over head-height so that with constant turning in different directions a person soon loses their sense of direction.

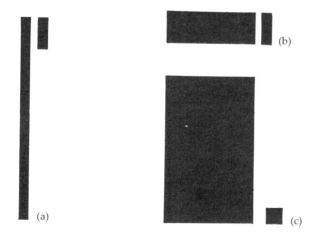

(a)

(b)

(c)

Three examples of typical size contrasts:
(a) long/short;
(b) wide/narrow;
(c) large/small.

Size is often thought of as absolute but in reality depends on a system of measurement to define it. Many measures are derived from the sizes of parts of the human body such as the forearm (cubit) and the joint of the thumb (inch). The size of units used in buildings for instance may be determined by the size of the hand (a brick), or by how much can be lifted by the technology available. This has an influence on the size of the building and its dimensions. Land measurement once depended on how much could be ploughed in a day (the acre) which influenced field sizes and thus landscape patterns.

Large, tall or deep forms tend to impress us since we compare them against our own size (see Scale). They may also seem endowed with splendour, majesty or in some other way seem awesome. The height and girth of a giant redwood tree, the height of a skyscraper, the lofty space inside the nave of a gothic cathedral, the depth of the Grand Canyon are examples of this.

Large size has also been consciously used by rulers to exert power over people by being able to demonstrate physical or

The Grand Canyon in Arizona is an example of a very deep open volume, impressive, awesome and dramatic. We feel dwarfed and vulnerable standing on its edge. (Courtesy of Maggie Gilvray.)

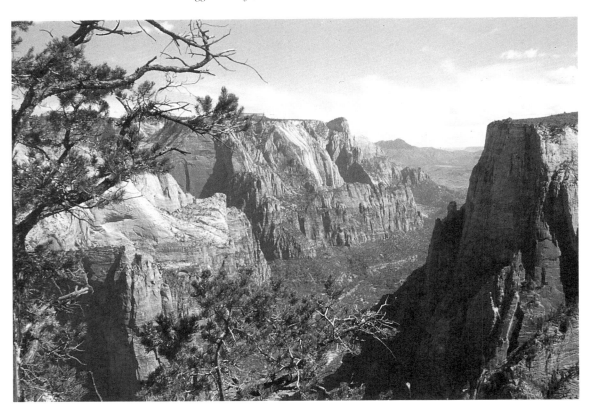

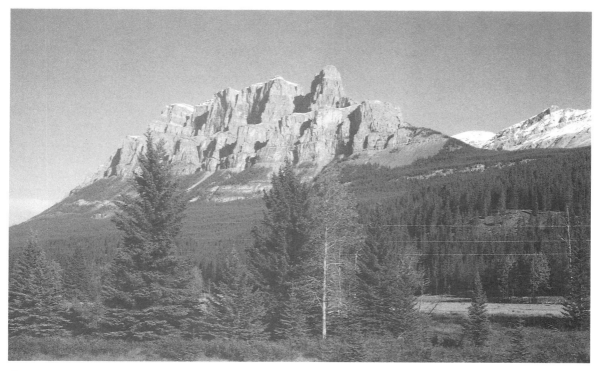

Castle Mountain near Banff in the Canadian Rockies is an example of a large solid volume – also impressive, perhaps remote, certainly dramatic.

This wall, a remnant of the once mighty citadel of Mycenae in Greece, is constructed of huge stones, carefully shaped and bedded into an interlocking pattern. Later generations thought that such walls could only have been raised by giants – the Cyclops – hence a mythology arose surrounding the place.

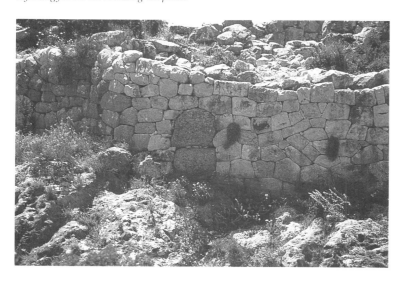

psychological dominance. The size of a castle or fortification was as much meant to overawe any attacker as provide real strength. The Tower of Babel needed to be tall in order to reach Heaven.

Smallness, on the other hand, is not impressive but has its own virtues. 'Small is beautiful' extols the benefits of not being dominant or unwieldy. A number of smaller elements may have less visual impact than one larger one: for example, lots of small houses instead of one tall block of flats.

The size of animals and plants is determined by natural forces or genetics. For example, insects are largely limited by their respiration system from growing any bigger. Trees may stop growing because of wind or decay. Food or nutrient shortages may prevent the achievement of maximum potential size.

Shape (form)

- Shape is one of the most important variables.
- Lines, planes and volumes all have shapes.
- Shapes range from simple and geometric to organic and complex.
- Compatibility of shapes is important for design unity.
- Natural shapes are usually irregular but some are geometric at a small scale.
- Plants, especially trees, display a wide range of shape and form.
- Buildings are more commonly composed of geometric forms but organic designs can be found.
- Geometric and organic forms can be mixed to produce interesting effects.

Shape is one of the most important variables and has particularly powerful and evocative effects on the way we perceive our surroundings as patterns. Shape is concerned with the variation of lines and the edges of planes and volumes (form is the three-dimensional equivalent of shape). It is the primary means by which we identify an element. It is such a powerful factor that we only need an outline or silhouette in order to recognize many three-dimensional forms. In other words, we can remove all the other features of an object leaving the basic shape and we still recognize it.

Linear shapes may be straight or curved or a combination of a number of straights and curves or both. They may be regularly or irregularly geometric or naturally irregular. Many natural lines are found in the landscape and only rarely are any of these straight or otherwise geometric. Usually they are irregularly curvilinear. This aspect is important because compatibility of

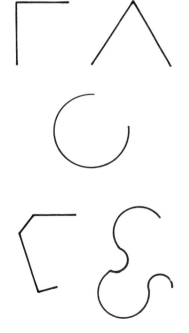

Some examples of geometric linear shapes.

shape is a major attribute of design unity. An incompatible shape, for example one which is curvilinear when the rest are straight, will tend to induce tension and visual conflict.

The shapes of planes compound the effect of lines. Once again, geometry has a major influence. Regular geometric planes are Euclidean polygons – the square, triangle, circle, hexagon, rhombus. Planes can also exhibit irregular geometry either by being compounds of regular shapes or by being asymmetric. Further variations include shapes combining curving and straight edges.

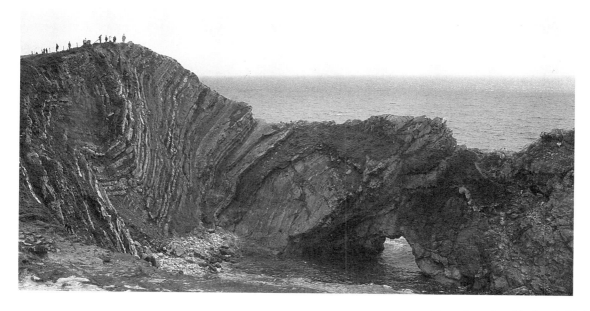

Linear shapes found in these twisted, arched and folded rock strata revealed by erosion at Lulworth Cove, Dorset, England.

A sinuous line of a road winding across an undulating landscape: its shape is compatible with the landform and so no tensions are created. South Dakota, USA.

Shape (form)

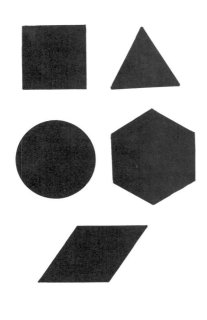

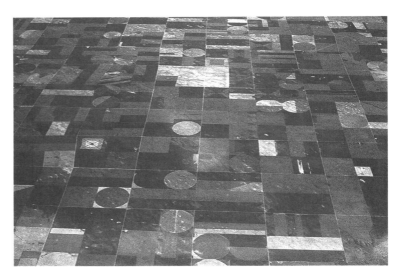

A highly geometric cultivation pattern in Nebraska, USA, seen from the air. The squares are derived from the land division of the Jeffersonian Grid while the circles are the result of irrigation systems.

A geometrically shaped plantation in the Black Mountains in Wales. Here the geometry is on two levels: the main woodland and the details of the 'castellation' along its upper edge and the contrasting species shapes within. The incompatibility of these shapes is particularly striking when seen alongside the adjacent, semi-natural vegetation patterns.

Examples of geometric planar shapes:
   (a) regular;
   (b) irregular.

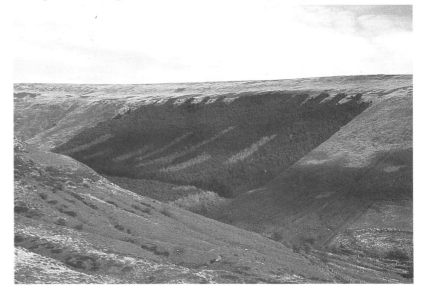

Natural irregular shapes are normally the antithesis of geometric ones. Usually they are less well defined, may be more difficult to identify and may resemble organic shapes, that is shapes whose origins lie in the results of the growth of living organisms.

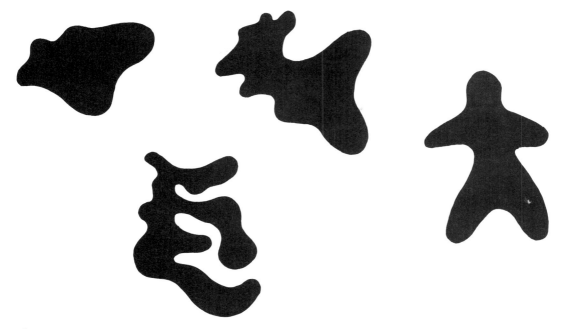

Irregular, organic and anthropomorphic planar shapes.

A woodland on the slopes above Loch Lomond, Scotland. Here the semi-natural nature of the woodland has resulted in a very irregular, diffuse shape to the edge which gradually blends into the open land above (see Density, Transformation).

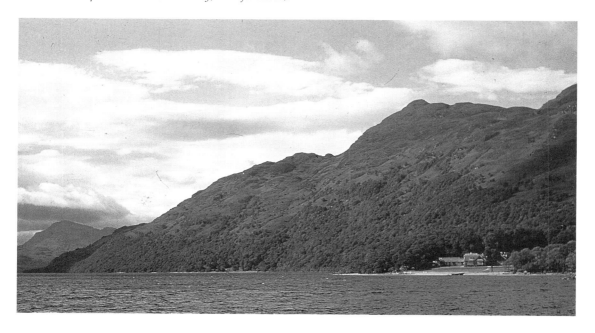

Shape (form)

As the complexity of shapes increases we may see the same portion of a shape repeated at different scales or at variable viewing distances.

As with lines, compatibility of planar shapes is important for design unity. Usually a consistency of shape or a gradual change from one type to another is necessary (see Transformation) unless, of course, a conscious contrast between shapes is a design objective.

Since shape is so powerful, our eyes tend to try and detect shapes in the landscape often on the slightest evidence. Three trees in a field may be enough to suggest a triangle; four a square, rhombus or trapezium.

Natural shapes need not always be irregular, nor repeat shapes at varying scales. Often they show an astonishing degree of symmetry at a small scale which is not usually maintained as the scale or size increases. For example, leaves may have very

Irregular fields in the Connemara landscape of the west of Ireland. Here the enclosures happened gradually without a pre-ordained plan which produces a more varied pattern of shapes on the hillside.

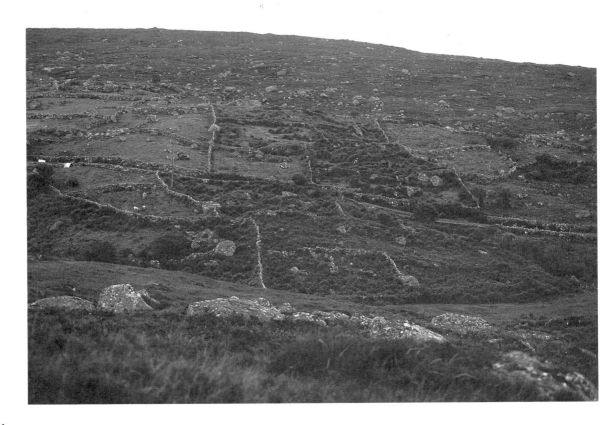

regular symmetrical shapes but the complete tree probably has an irregular outline due to wind, climate, soil and other pressures. A section of honeycomb may display remarkable geometric qualities of perfectly interlocking hexagons but the complete comb is likely to be irregular in order to fit an available space, perhaps the inside of a hollow tree.

Repeated natural shapes are often very similar to each other but not usually absolutely identical; ripple marks left in the sand are very similar in general but each one is slightly different; every snowflake is a six-pointed star but none are identical in shape (see Similarity).

The interaction of planar shapes with three-dimensional forms can produce interesting results. A regular, geometric pattern of fields or forest overlying an irregular landform can either appear distorted and therefore less regular or else the geometry may be as dominant as the landform, the resulting incompatibility causing visual disruption (see Visual force, Tension).

Three-dimensional forms have the same properties as lines or planes in the way that they can be geometric, irregular, organic.

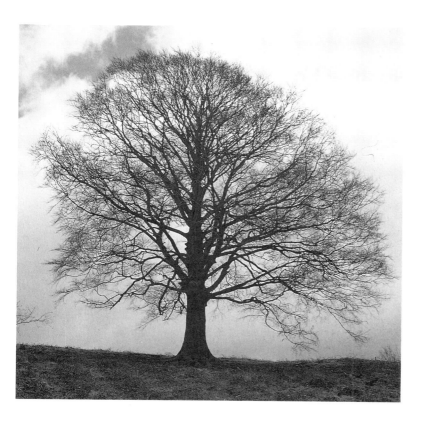

The shape of this tree seen in silhouette is made up of many irregular, twisting and criss-crossing, yet structured lines of branches.

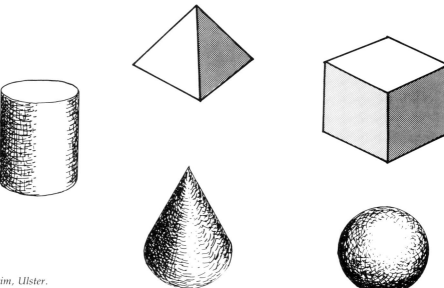

The Giant's Causeway, Co Antrim, Ulster. The pattern is made from more-or-less geometrically shaped hexagonal columns of basalt eroded into an irregular landform. (Courtesy of Alan Chalmers.)

Examples of geometric solid volumes.

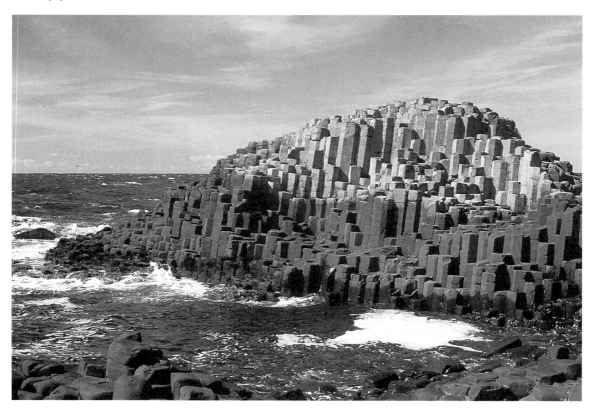

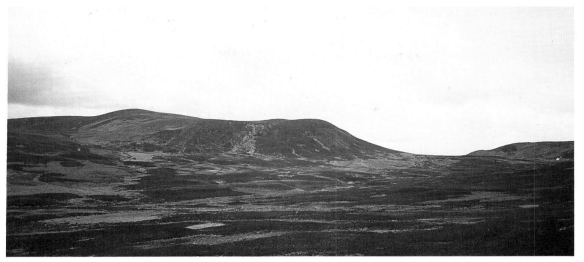

(a)

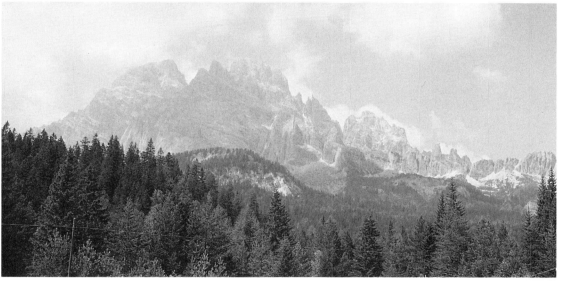

(b)

Natural geometric forms are relatively rare. They include crystals, the growth of molluscan shells and some rock features. The Giant's Causeway in Ulster is a good example of natural geometry. Owing to erosion landforms tend to be irregular. This may relate to the rock type, its hardness or softness or its strata, folding or faulting. The geological age of the landform may also make a difference to the type of shape. The relatively young mountain ranges of the Rockies, Andes, Alps and Himalayas display bigger, stronger, more jagged forms than the older, more eroded Appalachian or Caledonian mountains.

Trees and plants are further examples of natural forms. They differ between species – particularly whether conifer or broadleaf

Landforms can take on quite different shapes:
(a) a smooth, rounded, flowing landform in Sutherland, Scotland;
b) the Dolomites in northern Italy have prominent jagged shapes, hard and unfriendly.

57

Shape (form)

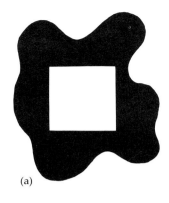

(a)

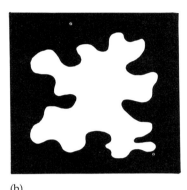

(b)

The interaction of irregular and regular shapes: (a) regular inside irregular; (b) irregular inside regular.

– and also at different ages. A young pine tree may have a very different form from an old one. Similarly, a tree grown in an open situation will look completely different from one grown in a wood. Some tree forms are particularly characteristic to certain species and can be recognized from their silhouettes.

Open volumes exhibit form in the same way as solids. The shape of a space can be geometric or irregular, straight or curving, reflecting the planes which form it or contrasting with them. Where a mass contains a void (an open volume within a solid one) they may be different, as in a cave within a hill or an irregular opening within a regularly shaped woodland. Conversely, the internal form may reflect the external one, as in many architectural examples: for instance St Paul's Cathedral in London where the external dome is reflected in the internal one although the latter is actually a false one.

Buildings tend to be predominantly composed of geometric forms – cubes, pyramids, spheres or segments of them – in various combinations. Some forms derive from the use of materials and their limitations, for example Eskimo igloos made of ice, while others have been developed from strictly functional requirements, such as power-station cooling towers. The designers of some other buildings have consciously used natural forms for their inspiration (See Case Study One). Sometimes the material used allows this, such as the fluid state of concrete before it sets which allows a wide range of different forms to be cast. The shell roofs at the Olympic Stadium in Montreal have a crustacean-like appearance exactly in keeping with their structure, a thin hard shell like a beetle's exoskeleton. The buildings of the Spanish architect Antonio Gaudi, although made of stone and brick, also have a certain fluid quality with curving, strongly organic shapes.

The shell roof of one of the stadia at the Olympic Park in Montreal, Canada. This has an organic, crustacean-like appearance constructed from thin, reinforced concrete. The ribs and rooflights contribute to its similarity to invertebrate form.

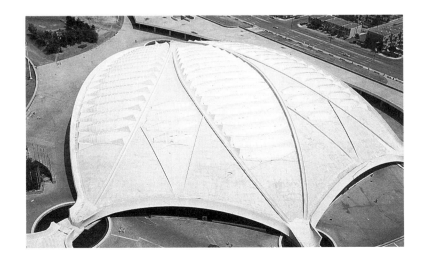

The juxtaposition of contrasting shapes can produce interesting results. Regular, rectangular elements such as paving units can be laid so that the overall shape of the paved area is organic or curvilinear, perhaps to emphasize the change from the formal design of a house to a less formal garden.

Interval

- Spacing between elements can be an integral part of design.
- Intervals can be equal or variable.
- Complex patterns of mixed intervals occur at varying scales.
- Interval can produce formal or informal patterns.
- Interval is a useful variable in design.
- Regular intervals are found in the layouts of many towns and cities.
- Buildings are often designed and constructed according to a grid of regular intervals.

The spacing between elements or component parts of an element may be an integral part of the way a design is put together. In fact it may be as important as the elements themselves.

Intervals can be equal or variable. An equal interval creates a sense of stability, regularity, perhaps formality. A variable interval can be either randomly derived or be generated by some sort of rule such as a mathematical progression. There can also be more complex patterns where clusters of elements separated by a short interval are themselves separated by wider intervals.

Interval is a useful variable with many applications because of the way it is connected with formality or informality. A regular arrangement of young trees planted in straight rows a set distance apart and equally spaced in the rows produces a strong impression of artificiality compared with the same trees more randomly scattered. Woodlands of great age are characterized, among other things, by the great variation in the spacing of the trees. As young woods planted in rows grow and become progressively thinned variability starts to increase.

Trees planted along hedgerows in Britain at the time of the enclosures were probably placed at regular intervals. With time and losses from death, decay and storms the spacing has become much less regular, looser and more informal.

Regular intervals are often found in the layout of built up areas. In great cities like Chicago which has been built on the 'Jeffersonian Grid' common to much of the United States the standard intervals between blocks extending over a large area and the lots within these blocks create a dominant pattern of regularity. Seen from the air this arrangement can seem inexorable (see Continui-

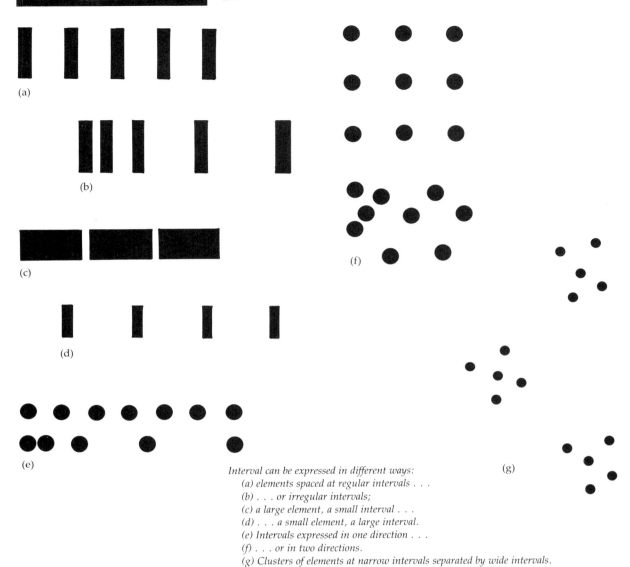

Interval can be expressed in different ways:
(a) elements spaced at regular intervals . . .
(b) . . . or irregular intervals;
(c) a large element, a small interval . . .
(d) . . . a small element, a large interval.
(e) Intervals expressed in one direction . . .
(f) . . . or in two directions.
(g) Clusters of elements at narrow intervals separated by wide intervals.

ty). The older industrial cities of Britain had large areas of terraced houses, all aligned in the same way and all at standard intervals apart. The apparent relentlessness of much recent housing anywhere is in part due to the near-standard spacing (as standard as land ownership and landform will allow) between houses.

Much architecture, whether classical or modern, relies on a grid set at a specific interval to determine its form and structure as well as the scale. The spacing of columns in a Doric temple, the façade of a Palladian villa or the layout of a building such as the Pompidou Centre in Paris, as well as countless office blocks, are examples of this approach.

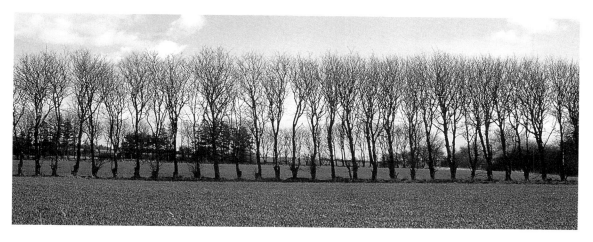

A row of trees planted at equal intervals for a wind break in Jutland, Denmark. The regularity of the tree size combines with the regularity of spacing to produce a somewhat formal result.

Trees along hedgerows in the Cotswold hills of England arranged with a more irregular, random interval between them achieve a less formal effect, the more so because of their variable size and shape.

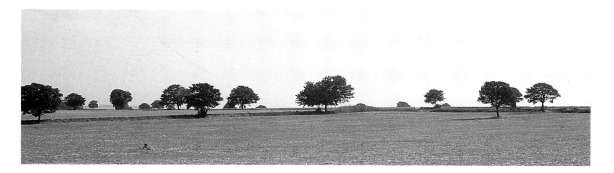

Texture

- Texture is related to interval.
- Texture depends on the sizes of elements and the intervals between them.
- Texture is relative, ranging from fine to coarse.
- Texture varies when seen at different distances enabling several textures to coexist simultaneously.
- Plants have different textures both in their constituent parts and in their whole appearance.
- Land-use patterns show a range of textures or grain.
- Built-up areas can also be seen as textures at particular viewing distances.

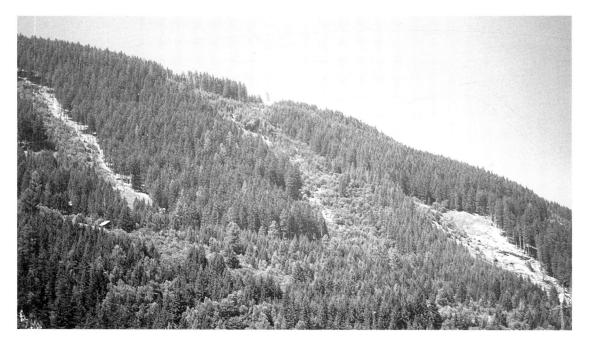

These three 'strip shelterwood' fellings, designed to regenerate the forest, are positioned at regular intervals across this mountainside in Austria. As time goes on further strips will be felled alongside the existing ones so that the pattern will march across the face and a striped effect will result. When the strips run perpendicularly up and down the hill like this, visual tension between the pattern and the natural landform or forest patterns can result.

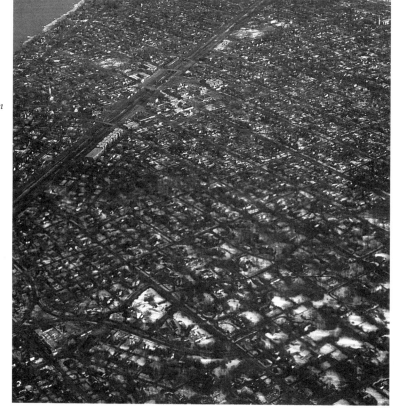

The pattern of this urban layout in the suburbs of Chicago is dependent on more-or-less equal intervals between the units of land ownership and the road layout. This is based on the Jeffersonian Grid and is only broken by later additions such as the freeway, or the edge of the lake. This pattern extends for many miles with the interval repeated over and over again (see Continuity).

A close relative of interval, texture refers to the visual and tactile effects of the spacing between elements as part of a much wider pattern and often at a smaller scale. Texture depends on the size of the element in relation to the size of the interval. All textures are relative. They depend on the distance of the viewer from the object for their effect and may change dramatically as distance varies. Often one texture seen close to may become part of a wider texture when seen from further away.

Textures range from fine – small elements at short intervals – to coarse – large elements at wider intervals. Many designs or landscapes are composed of planes whose surfaces display different textures. These may contrast with each other to produce interesting variety. This variety may be more expressive if related to the function of the different planes such as roof/wall, road/path, field/forest/moor.

Buildings usually show different textures between roof and wall, between windows/solid wall and between materials such as brick/stone/boarding. The layers of texture then become apparent starting with the basic material and working up to the scale of the entire building. For example, brick has a wide range of textures – smooth, rough, soft, hard, machine-finished or hand-made. Next the bonding pattern creates a texture together with the size of brick and the thickness of the mortar. Recessed joints producing shadow lines will have a different effect from flush joints. Whether the wall is flat-faced or whether it has recessed or protruding sections will alter the texture seen from further away as will any window pattern. A more distant view still may reveal the wall as a section of a much larger texture or grain as part of a large building or series of buildings.

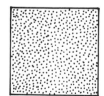 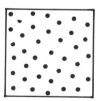 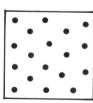

In each of these examples the texture is graded from fine to coarse as the size of the elements and the interval between them increases.

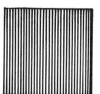  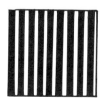

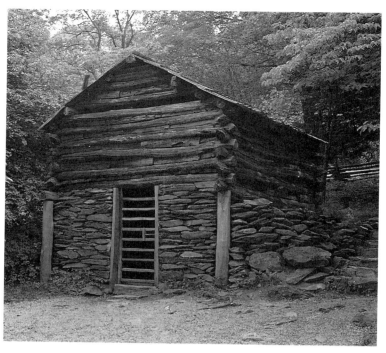

This small building on the Blue Ridge Parkway in Virginia, USA displays several textures which are derived from the materials and their inherent textures and the way they are used. The upper part of the wall, thick logs arranged at wide intervals, provides the coarsest texture, while the rubble wall to the right is less coarse but coarser than the wall to the left. Here the stones are more tightly bedded and tend to be smaller. The gravel of the yard is finest of all.

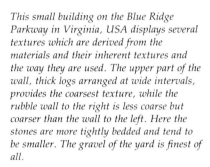

Plant textures are derived from the size, shape and interval of the stems, leaves and flowers. Each leaf may have its own texture. Often this is tactile as well as visual. The bark on tree trunks also has a distinct texture due to fissuring or flaking. The arrangement of the parts of the plant may then combine to produce an overall texture. Mixing plants of different textures in a design can thus be very effective.

Trees display textures in the same way as other plants but at a larger scale. The size of branches and the branching habit produce particular textures. In deciduous broadleaves these show up well in the winter. In the summer the leaves also contribute to texture. For example, horse chestnut has a coarse branching habit, rough fissured bark, large, rough leaves arranged at wide intervals which gives it a coarse texture overall. Beech, by contrast, has finer, more delicate branching, smooth bark and smaller, smoother leaves arranged in a close pattern producing a fine texture.

Conifers have very distinctive textures as a result of the normally much more regular branching patterns when compared with broadleaves. Many are quite stiff, with wide, regularly spaced whorls of branches and coarse needles. Firs and spruces are examples of this type. By contrast, cypresses have a very tightly packed crown made from smaller leaves and a very fine texture. Pines are somewhere in between.

Trees *en masse* show strong textural differences, particularly between conifers and broadleaves but also between different ages as well as the species differences described above. Younger trees at closer spacings tend to have finer textures than larger, older trees at wider spacings. Distance also plays a part, forests tending to look finer further away and coarser closer to. At a certain distance, the spaces in the forest – open ground or felled areas – also become part of the texture.

Farmed landscapes show textures in the cultivation patterns of different fields, crops and methods of harvesting. Ploughing produces quite a coarse texture which becomes finer after

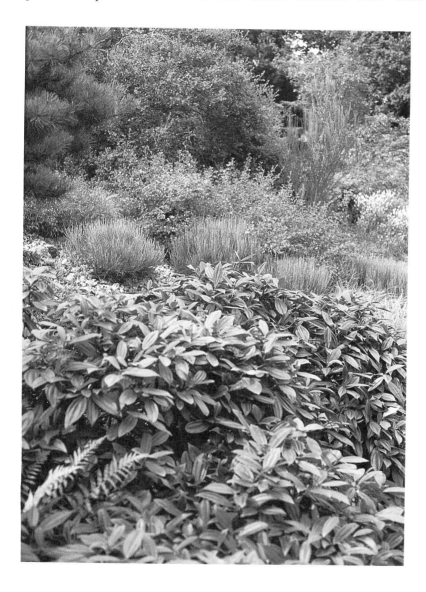

This bed at Hidcote Manor in Gloucestershire, England, shows a range of textures comprising leaf and branch size and interval. There are also textures to some of the leaves due to the pattern of veins.

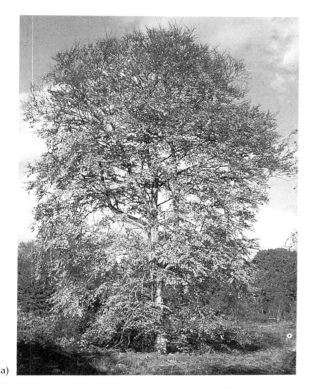

(a)

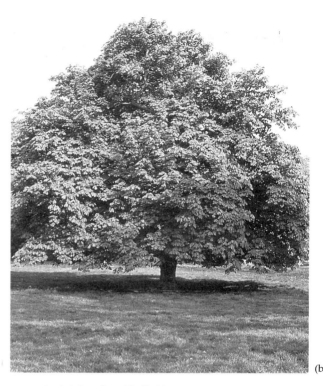

(b)

Trees exhibit different textures in their branch and leaf habits.
(a) A beech tree has smooth bark, small leaves finely arranged and a delicate branching habit producing a fine texture overall.
(b) By contrast a horse chestnut has rough bark, large, rough leaves and a coarse branching habit giving it an overall coarse texture.

harrowing. A combine harvester leaves swathes of straw behind which create a coarser texture than the original ploughing. At the next level are textures created by the field patterns and any enclosures such as hedges and trees. In England, the texture or grain of many farmed landscapes has coarsened over the last twenty years as hedgerows have been removed and field sizes have increased (see Diversity). In other parts of the world different crops produce a range of textures. In parts of the USA dry farming produces patterns of contour ploughing and strips of alternate crops which are both very distinctive and a response to particular conditions, namely soil erosion. Vines on the sunny side of the Mosel river in Germany produce a texture which is absent from the shady side where the vines will not grow. In tea-growing areas the fact that the tea bushes are constantly being picked leads to extensive areas of distinctive smooth texture.

Seen at a larger scale or over a wider distance still there are further textural contrasts between different land uses such as

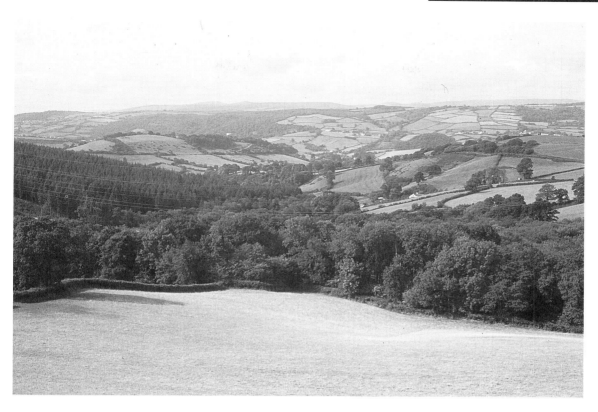

In this example from Devon in England, the textures vary greatly. In the foreground the fine texture of the grass, medium texture of the conifer woodland and the coarser texture of the broadleaved woodland contrast with each other. In the middle distance the texture of the individual fields reads as fine with the pattern of field enclosures beginning to assert itself, whereas in the background it is the grain of the landscape, the broader texture of fields, hedges, trees and woods which stands out. The removal of some elements such as hedges would tend to coarsen the texture overall.

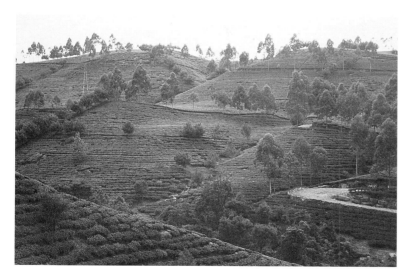

The bushes on this Sri Lankan tea plantation are plucked every few days so that they have a very fine texture. Since the bushes are planted closely together the texture is continuous over whole hillsides, the only variation being the access roads and the clumps of trees.

farmland and moorland, enclosed pasture and designed parkland. These patterns are related functionally as well as visually.

Seen from an elevated viewpoint a city can be seen to have a texture or grain which will vary depending on the density of the buildings. An older, higher-density layout of similar-sized houses with similar roof materials has a fine texture compared with a low-density area of large buildings which has a coarser texture.

Density

- Density is related to interval and texture.
- Gradations of density are common in transitional zones between land use or vegetation types.
- Urban landscapes show density patterns related to function.

Related to interval and texture, density refers to the number of units of an element within a given area such as on the surface of a plane. Density may vary across the pattern. Areas of greater density tend to have greater visual weight. Examples of this might be clusters of points or tonal shadings.

Textural density variations are often seen at junctions between two types. This can be seen where woodland gives way to open ground where a gradual decrease in the density of the trees occurs, from solid cover to mostly solid but with some openings, then increasingly patchy cover until almost completely open with isolated trees and eventually treeless altogether. This gradation is

This view of Venice, seen from a high point, shows how the repeated, similar forms of the buildings at similar narrow intervals create a grain or texture across the city. This provides a background from which larger, more prominent structures rise (see Figure and Ground).

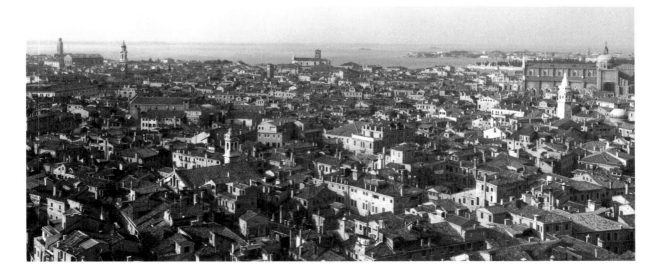

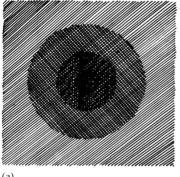

(a)

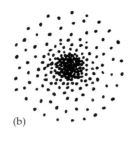

(b)

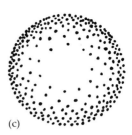

(c)

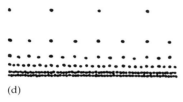

(d)

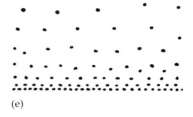

(e)

Some examples of density patterns.
   (a) Density increases towards the centre of the diagram as the interval between the lines decreases.
   (b) This pattern is denser towards the middle with decreasing interval . . .
   (c) . . . while this increases towards the edges.
   (d) Density can decrease in a regular . . .
   (e) . . . or in an irregular fashion.

not usually regular but varies according to local site conditions such as soil or shelter, and over different distances can be seen to be repeated.

Density gradients can be seen at a larger scale in land-use patterns. The change from small, intensively cultivated fields with smooth texture through larger-sized ones with rougher vegetation and on to open moorland produces a pattern related both to the scale of the landscape and to agricultural practice (see Transformation).

Another density gradient can be seen in semi-arid areas where vegetation tends to be more concentrated in the bottom of valleys where there are moister conditions, and sparser on drier areas such as knolls. Such gradients are not always static. They may change with climatic patterns as in the case of forest and bog margins where in wetter periods the bog tends to advance and grow at the expense of the trees and vice versa in drier times when the forest spreads on to the bog.

Density patterns in natural systems such as boglands may produce very interesting patterns at different scales where open pools of water are clustered in groups.

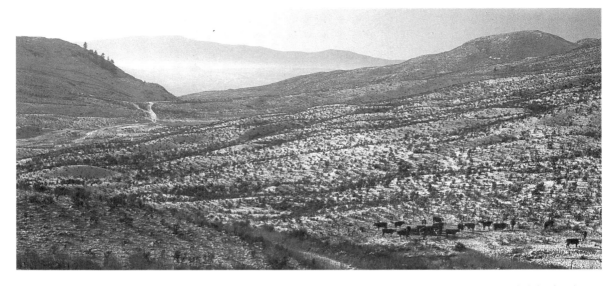

The vegetation patterns in this ranching landscape near Kamloops, British Columbia shows definite density gradients related to the local landform; the density is greater in the hollows where there is more moisture, and sparser on the dry ridges and knolls.

The pattern of Dubh Lochans (Black Pools) in the Flow Country of Caithness, Scotland. Here the pools are clustered together in denser groups separated by wider intervals.

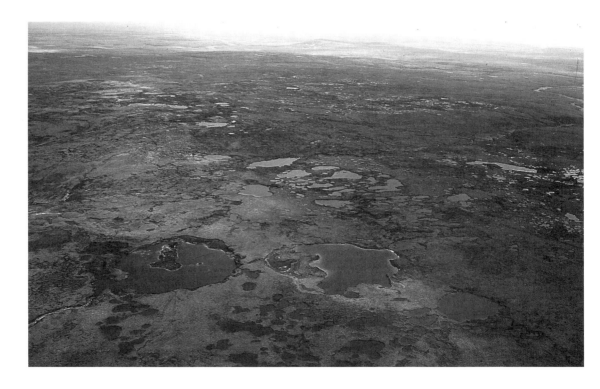

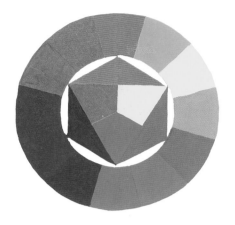

Plate 1
The colour circle; primaries in the centre,
secondaries next and a range of spectrum or
tertiaries arranged around the outside.

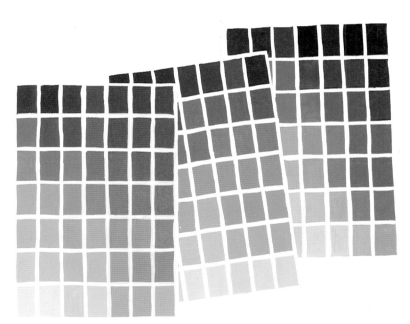

Plate 2
A sample of colours arranged and varied
according to hue, lightness/value and
saturation/chroma. Value is arranged up
and down the rows, the columns represent
increasing/decreasing saturation/chroma
level and each card is of a different hue.

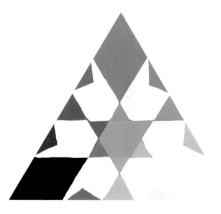

Plate 3
A colour triangle showing gradation of a
hue based on tones and tints.

Plate 4
A scene in Tuscany, Italy where the colours are distinctive to the area and occur in a complementary relationship: the orange/red of the tiles and brickwork harmonizes with the grey/green olives and the darker green of the other trees.

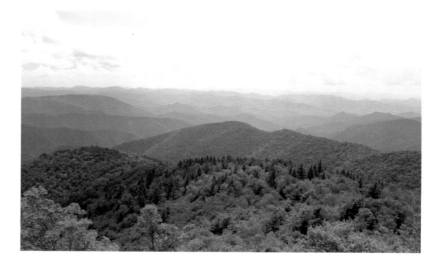

Plate 5
Atmospheric perspective: the landscape appears bluer as distance from the viewer increases. Here the Blue Ridge Mountains take their name from this phenomenon.

Plate 6
A cluster of farm buildings in Alberta. The ox-blood red of the walls harmonizes with the generally green landscape. The reflective light-coloured roofs provide a strong contrast and draw the eye to them. The roofs tend to seem larger and the building seems less attached to the ground as a result.

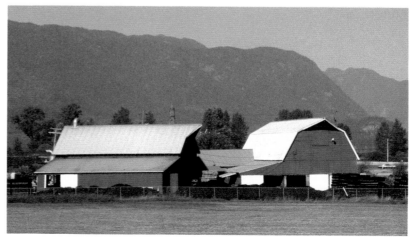

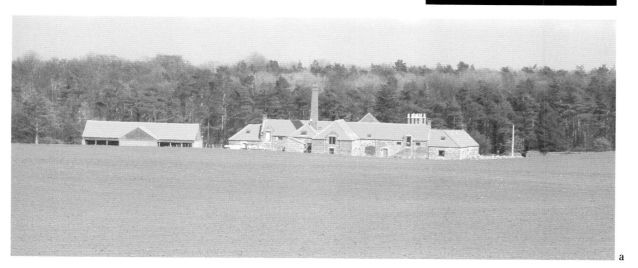

a

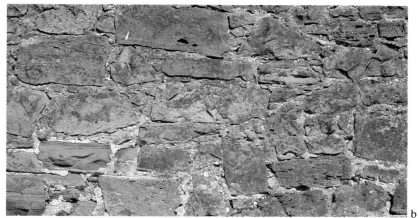

b

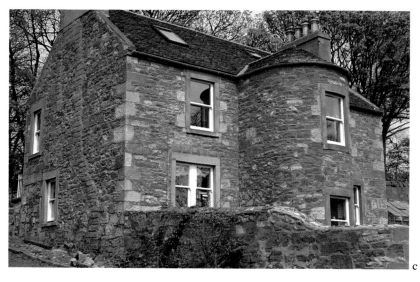

c

Plate 7
(a) Reddish brown soil derived from Old Red Sandstone is characteristic of East Lothian in Scotland.
(b) A close-up of a wall built from the local stone reveals the dominant pinkish-red hues present.
(c) A house built of the local stone contains some variety in the range of pinks, reds and browns.

Plate 8
Colonial Williamsburg, Virginia, USA.
The clapboard houses are all painted using
original colours once traditional in the area.
Here a sage green contrasts nicely with the
white frames, brown doors and reddish
brown brick of the chimney.

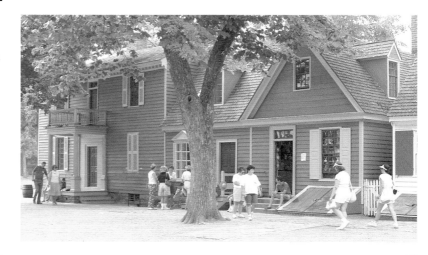

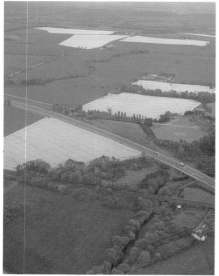

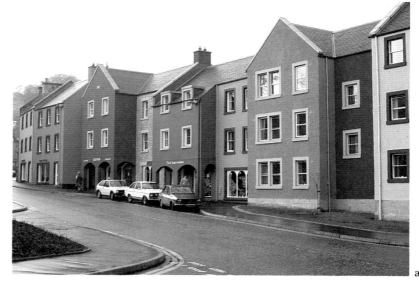

Plate 9
In this view the intense chroma of the
yellow oilseed rape stands out strongly
amongst the less saturated greens which
otherwise predominate in the landscape.
This effect can be highly intrusive,
especially since the yellow is rather crude. A
more orange hue would be easier to
accommodate.

Plate 10
(a) This group of houses has been painted
in a range of hues traditional to the area
and balanced into asymmetric amounts
along the façades.
(b) An anlysis in monochrome shows
that a balance in value can also be
achieved as well as hue and chroma.

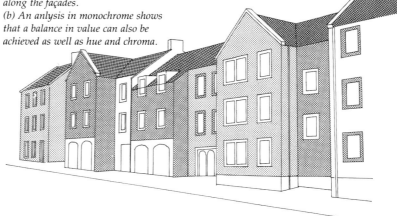

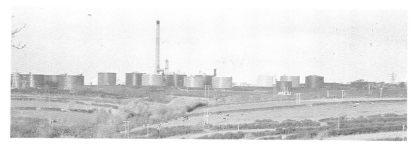

Plate 11
A large oil tank farm at Milford Haven, Pembrokeshire, Wales. The tanks have been painted a range of receding colours, some to create shadow effects. The one red tank acts as a focal point (an accent colour) which draws the eye and helps pull the composition together. (Courtesy of Ray Perry.)

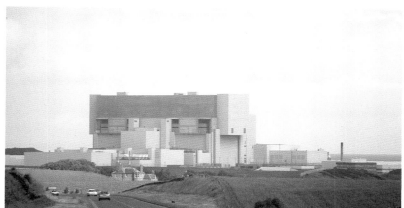

Plate 12
A large power station which has been painted a soft blue-grey to try to dilute the mass seen against the sky in this coastal location. The result is quite successful in weather similar to that present when the photograph was taken. A darker colour would emphasize the silhouette while a lighter one would be too reflective and cause the building to seem even larger. The simple design means that the true size of the building is difficult to judge (see Scale).

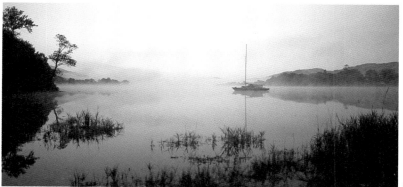

Plate 13
Diurnal changes in the landscape:
(a) dawn with mist;
(b) dusk where the rosy light reflects on the water of Lake Coniston in Cumbria, England. (Courtesy of Oliver Lucas.)

a

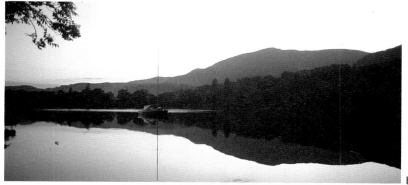

b

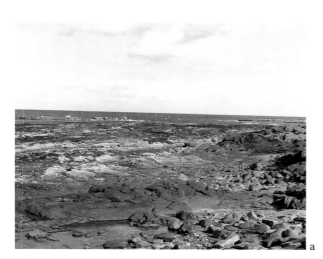

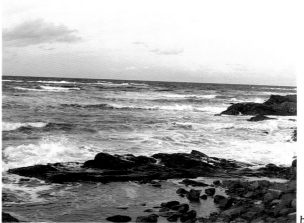

Plate 14
Other diurnal changes include the tides:
   (a) low tide – the foreshore, rock pools and beach exposed;
   (b) high tide – waves washing on to the foot of the rocks.

a

b

Plate 15
Seasonal changes are one of the main cycles which affect the landscape:
   (a) spring, with new growth and fresh leaves;
   (b) summer, where darker greens, deeper shadows and a sense of maturity are dominant;
   (c) autumn, when rich hues colour the scene;
   (d) winter, when snow covers up surface patterns and transforms the landscape.

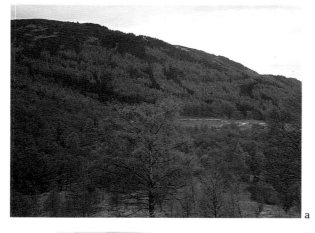

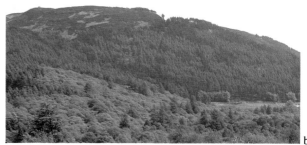

a

b

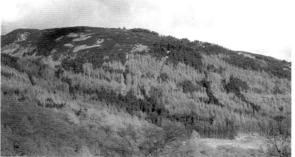

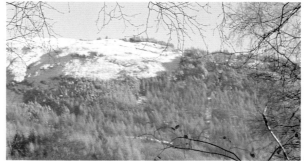

c

d

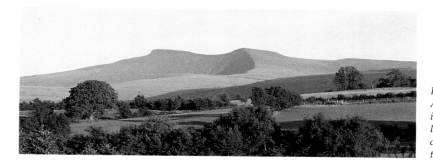

Plate 16
A side-lit landscape in the Brecon Beacons in Wales. The sculptural qualities of the landscape are revealed by the deep shadow cast into the hollow on the northern slope of the hill.

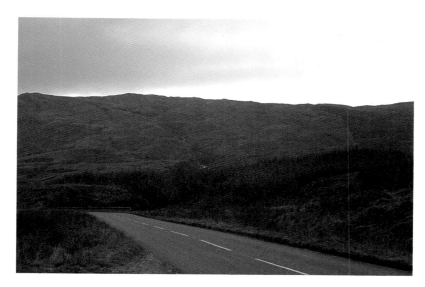

Plate 17
A back-lit landscape where the skyline dominates and all detail is lost on the shaded face of the hill.

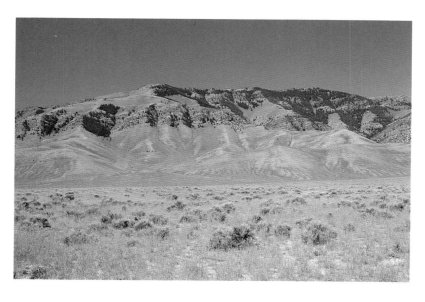

Plate 18
A front-lit landscape in Idaho, USA where the colours of soil and vegetation show up but where the lack of shadows flattens out our sense of the landform.

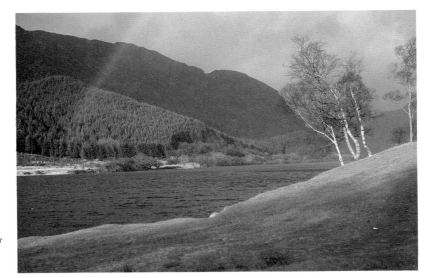

Plate 19
This scene catches the special qualities associated with a storm – the highlighting of parts of the landscape, the dark shadows of others, and the rainbow.

Plate 20
The same scene, a street in Niagara Falls, Ontario, Canada:
(a) by daylight – a tawdry effect, far from romantic and . . .
(b) by night where the glamorous effects transform the street into an exciting place.

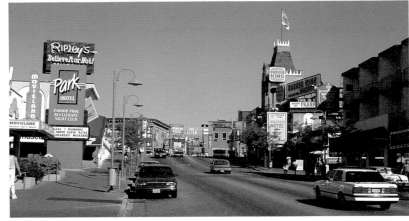

a

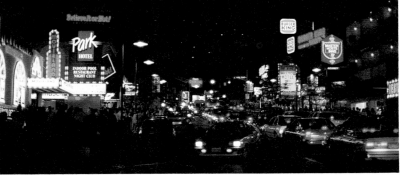

b

Urban areas often display striking density variations. Large cities often have their denser, high-rise development concentrated in one central zone while the urban fabric gradually reduces in density out from these nodes, from business towards residential areas. In the largest conurbations there may be several such density nodes joined by continuous, less dense, built up areas.

As a design tool density provides a good way to handle changes in texture where a gradation is preferred over abrupt transitions. In nature these gradients tend to be normal and can be emulated by design. Density can also be of use when fitting a new building development into an existing pattern where it is desirable to blend it into the overall texture.

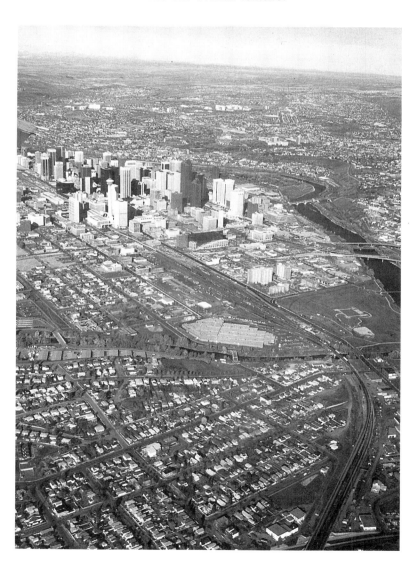

Calgary, Alberta, is a city where the urban development shows a strong density gradient from the main business district downtown, with clusters of tall buildings, to the lower-density suburbs. There are several lesser nuclei further out from the centre representing neighbourhood centres.

Colour

- There are several methods of organizing and describing colour.
- A colour circle is a good arrangement to show the relationships between different colours.
- Colours are further described by *hue*, *lightness* and *saturation*. The Munsell system is a commonly used example.
- Certain colours can also be described as warm or cool, advancing or receding while blueness is associated with distance.
- Dark colours seem to occupy less space than light colours and seem heavier.
- Landscapes tend to be associated with a particular limited range of colours, helping to give them local identity.
- Colours found in the landscape may be used to create a palette for colouring man-made structures.
- Large structures may be visually detached from the earth by using paler sky tones.

As one of the most important variables related primarily to the surfaces of planes and volumes, colour has received much specialist attention. The physical and optical properties of colour have also been well researched and deeply studied ever since Newton discovered the prism and determined the visible spectrum. In visual design it is important to understand how to describe colour, what its properties are and some of the effects which occur or can be created.

Colours can be basically organized into three types – primaries, secondaries and tertiaries. In terms of coloured light there are three primaries – *red*, *green* and *blue* – which, when combined as pairs, produce secondary colours and, when all three are mixed, pure white.

Primary colours using pigments are different. They are *magenta*, *cyan* and *yellow*. Mix any two and secondaries result; mix two secondaries to obtain tertiaries.

The well-known rainbow spectrum of colour produced by splitting white light through a prism is the basis for all arrangements of colour. Normally a colour circle is used since the colours at the opposite ends of the spectrum are visually closely related. The circle can be analysed to determine various relationships between the colours (Plate 1).

Colours immediately adjacent to each other in the circle are known as *similar* colours and they tend to harmonize with each other. This is because their wavelengths are similar. They also tend to be from either the 'warm' or 'cool' part of the spectrum and so provoke emotional responses (see below).

Colours opposite each other in the circle also harmonize and are known as *complementary* colours. These are normally pairs of warm and cool colours which create a visually balanced effect. A simple test of complementary colours is to stare for several seconds at a strongly coloured object, for example, something bright green. On suddenly looking away at a white surface an 'after image' of the object in red or pink will fleetingly appear. A further harmony occurs by mixing split complementaries. Here one colour is set against the two adjacents to the complementary to create a more refined and subtle harmony.

In nature arrangements of similar colours are common such as the reds, oranges and yellows of a rich sunset or the oranges, yellows and browns of autumn leaves. Similar colours often grade from one to another: for example, a flower will grade from, say, blue at the outer tips of the petals through to deep purple towards the centre. Complementary harmonies are also to be found in flowers where violet blooms will often have a yellow centre. Deep blue skies seen with the orange glow of sunset; orange and red autumn leaves seen against bluish-green conifers; the orange and blue plumage of a kingfisher are other examples of complementary relationships.

Triads are harmonies of three colours – the three primaries, three secondaries or two sets of intermediates – all separated by 30 degrees across the circle.

Problems occur when colours not directly opposite across the circle or at least one segment removed from the adjacent are mixed. Then they clash; the greater the divergence from the harmony, the greater the discord will appear.

The combination of pigmented colours seen in different-coloured light can produce complex effects. A further harmonizing effect can occur when the rosy glow of sunset washes all surfaces with the same light, smoothing out otherwise discordant effects.

Colour can be arranged in more ways than the basic colour wheel described above. Several systems have been developed but most use the three-way organization of *hue, lightness/value* and *saturation/chroma*. A colour can be varied according to one of these methods in an almost infinite number of ways, although the eye can only differentiate between some thousands.

One commonly used arrangement is that based on the Munsell system (named after Alfred Munsell who developed it in 1915). This arranges different colours (hues) vertically according to the spectrum; each hue is then ranged for lightness to darkness (value) across a series of steps. Saturation or chroma, which refers to the strength of the colour (or conversely to the amount of greyness in it), is arranged in batches of each hue and value range in a number of degrees of strength. Each of these variations is then given a number (hue, saturation group and value) making it possible to specify any of the several hundred colours precisely (Plate 2).

Colour balance can be achieved with other variables. One way is by separating a colour into tints, tones and shades. Here the pure colour is mixed with white to produce tints, black to produce shades and grey to produce tones (this can be shown arranged as a triangle). Some colour arrangements work best where one light colour is set against another deeper or darker one, rather than using pure (completely saturated) colours. This can be used to introduce a form of hierarchy into the colour scheme (Plate 3). 'Accent colours' are a well-known use of this principle where a small bright (highly saturated) colour is used on a detail to balance and contrast a much larger area of a darker or less saturated colour.

Colours have many attributes. Some create physical/visual sensations, others emotional ones. Colours in the red/orange/yellow range are known as advancing colours because they seem to stand out and move towards the viewer compared with colours in the blue/green range which appear to recede. This occurs because red or orange light is less scattered in the atmosphere than blue or green. The result can be seen in a red or orange object: for example a flower or small structure set against a predominately green background or together with blue objects. The red or orange feature will seem to stand out and appear closer to the viewer. Anything in an advancing colour tends to assert itself to us more readily than an object in a receding colour: hence the common use of such colours on signs (Plate 4).

Colours can be further described as 'warm' or 'cool'. Again, the differences are between the oranges and reds which are associated with warmth (the red glow of a fire) and blues with cold (ice and snow, shadows in moonlight). This can have a psychological effect on us: for example, if we move to a pale blue room on a very hot day we will instantly seem to feel cooler even if the temperature is much the same as outside.

Blueness is also associated with distance in the phenomenon known as aerial perspective. Because of dust and moisture in the atmosphere, distant parts of the landscape appear progressively bluer in colour until they merge into the sky. The Blue Ridge Mountains in Virginia, USA are classic examples of this phenomenon (Plate 5).

Light and dark colours appear to occupy different amounts of space. Light colours, especially white, seem to spread out. Any light-coloured mass, such as the roof of a large building, will appear to be bigger than the same roof in a darker colour, an effect exaggerated by the higher reflectivity of roofs over walls. This effect can be used to reduce the apparent mass or size of large objects in the landscape by painting a large building, for instance, a darker colour.

Some colours also seem heavier or lighter than others. Once again it is the darker, green/brown colours which seem heavier than paler, bluer ones. A dark roof can cause a building to appear to sit more firmly on the ground than a light-coloured roof which may seem to float. This effect also depends on the value (lightness or darkness) of the colour in relation to the colour of the sky (Plate 6).

Colours can react together when mixed to produce a result different from the constituent parts. Small areas of different colour can appear to mix like light to create other colours. This is in part the result of the near simultaneous effect of the complementary after-image of each colour helping to blend them into a more even tone than the originals. This effect has been used by the Impressionist painters, especially the pointillists such as Seurat. It can also be seen when looking at a meadow full of different-coloured flowers which blend at a distance to produce a softer effect.

In the landscape, a very wide range of colours can be found, either naturally occurring or man-made. However, only a relatively small number are found together in any one place. There are great regional differences in colour due to the combinations of rock type, soil, vegetation and local building materials.

In some places the rock type and soils derived from it are particularly important contributors to the overall colour palette for an area (Plate 7). Old red sandstone in Devon or East Lothian in Scotland has produced deep reddish-brown soil and stone for buildings which almost seem to grow out of the earth. Slate areas such as North Wales are characterized by rock outcrops, buildings and many other objects (e.g. fences, gravestones) of the same dark purplish-grey stone. Oolitic limestone areas such as the Cotswolds feature the same honey-coloured stone in buildings and field walls.

Where stone is not so plentiful and timber has been used then colour is either that of the weathered wood, a pale grey, or some sort of paint or stain finish. Certain colour combinations are favoured in particular areas. Weatherboarding was typical in parts of south-east Britain from where it was taken by settlers to the USA. In New England and in particular in Virginia it has been and still is extensively used together with a range of traditional paint colours. These can be seen at Colonial Williamsburg in Virginia where the houses are painted using the pigments available in the eighteenth century, derived from natural materials. Seen in combination they produce a very harmonious effect (Plate 8).

Colour

In countries where the light tends to be strong, colours often tend to be brighter. In Brazil some towns are traditionally painted in very bright, almost gaudy colours. This is necessary in order for them to compete with the strong sunshine. In Greece whitewashed cottages are often decorated with strongly coloured doors and shutters, especially blue, in order to compensate for the high reflectivity of the white walls.

In nature, the strong highly saturated colours are seldom to be found in large quantities. Usually they belong to individual flowers and are more commonly found amongst other, duller colours, especially greens. In the tropics strong colours are more likely to be found than in higher latitudes where colours tend to be much more subdued. Cultivation has bred some strong colours among crops which are now seen in concentrations not usually found in nature. Oilseed rape and linseed, sunflowers, tulip fields or roses can present great swathes of colour at certain seasons of the year (Plate 9).

Forests tend to be quite subdued in colour except in autumn when leaf fall among deciduous forests can produce a blaze of reds and oranges. Vermont and other New England states are renowned for this. Winter colours tend to be much more washed out, in part due to lower sun angles and lower light levels.

Using colour can be a particularly creative part of design. Colour palettes for particular uses can be assembled either with reference to the basic rules of harmony described above, by researching and identifying the colours found in a particular landscape or a locality or a combination of the two.

Plants in garden design can be arranged to harmonize by any of the methods described above. Gertrude Jekyll's famous herbaceous borders were masterpieces of colour composition. Many modern plants have been bred for brighter, unusual colours which are more difficult to harmonize than the older varieties which were less strong and vivid in hue. The use of dominant tints can also help to harmonize colour. Silver- and grey-foliaged plants can provide a background against which to set a wider range of flower colours. The use of a single colour for the flowers will draw attention to the forms and textures of the foliage.

Harmonizing buildings in the landscape, especially larger ones, can be tackled in a number of ways. For those whose size is more in keeping with local buildings careful choice of materials or applied colour can be effected by sampling local materials and preparing a palette of colours so that the new will fit in with the old. It is important to establish the appropriate chroma and value as well as the hue and this can be done using monochrome sketches, for example, which omit hue and so concentrate on patterns of darkness and lightness, since it is often the case that insufficient differences between chroma and value are chosen than may be present in the surroundings (Plate 10).

For larger buildings the same methods can be used but if a reduction in apparent bulk is desired then the roof will need to be darker than the walls and strong, bright colours restricted to emphasize elements such as the doors or windows. This is common practice for treating large factory or farm buildings. For the latter the choice of colours may be determined from the range of colours found locally in the landscape, while factory buildings in urban areas may be treated in a more abstract fashion (Plate 11). Camouflage is the most extreme method of blending a large object into its surroundings, usually by using colour to break up its form as well as its mass.

Huge structures such as power stations are too big to blend into their surroundings and dark colours may emphasize their silhouette rather than reduce their bulk. Colour is then used to try to simplify the forms, to break the building mass into smaller parts. The form, usually the upper part, can also be diluted by choosing colours which may be borrowed from the sky or clouds (Plate 12). This technique appears to detach the building from the earth (the opposite of many other methods), and diffuse the mass into the sky, using the pale colour to increase its apparent lightness. Another technique is similar to camouflage in that an attempt is made to break down the form into a more abstract image of an indeterminate scale without necessarily blending it into its surroundings.

Time

- All objects or landscapes change over time.
- Time is marked in relation to natural cycles, the universe and our lives.
- Time can be registered as cyclical or progressive.
- Change occurs over variable time intervals.
- Seasons are one of the more important ways of dividing time.
- The life spans of humans, animals and plants are other registers of time.
- Time is also involved in motion and a moving observer's position.

So far we have examined basic elements in terms of their static physical attributes. All real objects change over time, the fourth dimension. We often judge the rate of change over time according to the various rhythms of the natural world, the universe and in relation to our own life span.

Time can be registered as being cyclical – the seasons, day and

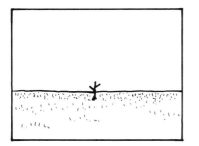

Time can be registered visually by the waxing and waning of the moon.

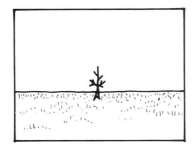
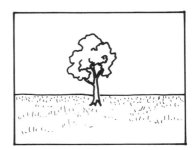
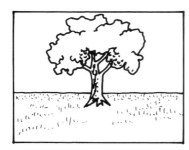
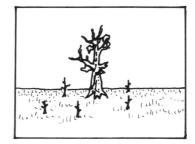

Time is also measured by growth and decay.

night – or progressive – birth, growth, decay, death. Time is related to motion as speed or velocity.

In the landscape some of the smallest or most rapid changes over time are those of the weather, especially in maritime climates. This can have a great effect on how we perceive a particular scene. Clouds scudding across the sky cause continuous changes in the light. Sudden breezes spring up and then die away, creating short-lived movement in trees, waves flowing across the grass and turning the calm surface of a lake into a minor storm.

Diurnal changes from dawn to noon, to dusk and on to night are accompanied by different light, our own pattern of activity and rest and those of other animals abroad or at rest at different times (Plate 13). The daily ebb and flow of the tides changes the landscape of the seashore (Plate 14).

There are monthly changes accompanied by the wax and wane of the moon. The weather may change, we may respond with different rhythms of activity or lethargy and each month brings subtle developments in growing plants, less obvious, perhaps, than the main seasonal divisions.

The seasons register change at a slower pace. The growth of plants, the appearance of decidous woods and trees and weather changes all characterize the seasonal cycle (Plate 15). This is more pronounced at high latitudes: for example in tundra regions where summers are short and growth and breeding are packed into a few short weeks of long days. In lower latitudes seasons are divided into wet or dry or monsoon periods. In equatorial areas growth may continue unabated all year round. Seasons are marked by migrations of birds, fish and animals as well as plant growth, flowering and fruiting. They are also the most culturally important cycles known to man. Festivals and religious rites have always been intimately associated with the seasons, especially those heralding the arrival of spring and the summer and winter solstices.

Life cycles are also important markers of time. Many insects have life cycles of a few weeks. Small mammals multiply over a summer and all but die out by the winter and following spring. At the other end of the scale tortoises and elephants may live much longer than a human life span, while trees are known to live for several hundreds or even thousands of years. This longevity can have a deep meaning for us. A sense of permanence and stability is suggested by a venerable oak tree or a giant redwood which has been known to several generations of people. The loss of such a tree in a storm, or by being felled, can be a quite traumatic event.

Woods and forests may have existed for much longer periods, even though the actual trees themselves have been replaced several times. There may be a mystical quality to the remnants of primeval forests which have been in existence since the ice ages, or for much longer in the case of tropical forests.

Time may also be registered in the accumulation of human remains and artefacts. Landscapes which contain relics from many ages provide a 'palimpsest' of man's activities in that place. In Britain an area may have Neolithic long barrows near to Bronze Age round barrows, Romano-British remains, an Anglo-Saxon church, a Norman castle and so on to the present day. In other parts of the world, such as the Near East and Mesopotamia, towns and villages may still exist on hills (tells) created from accumulated settlement remains dating back up to 8000 years.

When we look at a landscape, we are looking at something that is for ever changing both physically and visually. Hence the effects of growth and decay have to be taken into account in design not only where plants and other living things are concerned but also in buildings and in towns and cities. A design appears to belong to a place if it also respects and draws from the history recorded in the landscape (see *Genius loci*).

So far we have dealt with a changing landscape and a static viewer. However, time is also manifest in movement and speed of movement. The landscape is often observed from a moving position such as a car, train, aeroplane or by walking through it. Different speeds affect our perception. At fast speeds the eye is unable to register detail close to the observer and we tend to take in only the broader picture and focus on more distant parts of the landscape. The degree of variation of the landscape in relation to the speed of movement also makes a difference. In Britain it is possible to experience a great many landscape types in a day's drive; in the USA, especially in some plains states, a day's drive may involve hardly any change in the type of landscape (see Diversity).

Light

- We need light in order to perceive the environment.
- Light can be natural or artificial.
- The amount, quality and direction of light are important.
- Natural light contains all visible wavelengths.
- Light can be ambient or direct.
- Colour is dependent on light.
- Light quality involves the strength of the light and clarity of the atmosphere and is one important variable.
- Lighting direction is the other variable, whether side, back, front or top lit.
- Artificial light gives complete control over any desired effects.

We cannot see our environment unless it is lit in some way, either by natural or artificial means. The amount, quality and direction of the light have a major effect on our perception of shape and form, texture and colour.

Natural light, usually sunlight but also including moonlight, which is reflected sunlight, contains the complete range of visible wavelengths. Ambient light refers to the general all-pervasive outdoor light present even on dull days when the sun is obscured behind thick cloud. It casts no shadows and is fairly flat and even. Direct light from the sun or an artificial light source is usually brighter and casts shadows, thus giving form to three-dimensional objects.

True colour is dependent on natural, unfiltered light. Light which has been filtered to remove one or more visible component of the spectrum will produce an altered colour. So will any

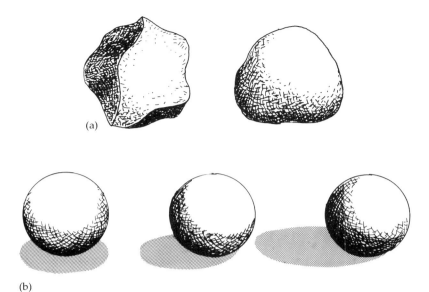

(a)

(b)

(a) Light gives three dimensions and form to objects.
(b) The angle of light causes shadows to fall in different places and cast different parts of the object in shade.

artificial light unless produced to reflect the composition of natural light. The amount of light in any particular place depends on the time of year, amount of cloud cover, time of day and degree of shade cast by an object.

The quality of light varies depending on a number of factors. In high latitudes where the angle of the sun is lower the light is not nearly as strong as in lower latitudes where the sun is more or less overhead. In cloudy conditions the strength is reduced and the light is diffused and scattered, reflection is less and the light is softer. Moisture in the atmosphere below the cloud level also causes further diffusion. This can create particular effects in high latitudes, especially in coastal areas such as in the west of Scotland, Ireland or British Columbia, where the light seems especially bright and clean.

Smog in some areas also has a marked effect, reducing clarity and increasing diffusion. In cloudless and dry climates therefore the light tends to be harsh, washing out the colour (in reality an effect of the light strength on the retina of the eye), and produces strong, well-defined shadows. Glare, light reflected from surfaces, is also produced making it painful for the eyes to look at light-coloured objects. In such circumstances we tend to see shadows as distinctly bluish in colour.

The colours used in particular areas, for example on houses, often bear a relationship to the light quality. Muted tones are

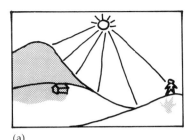

(a)

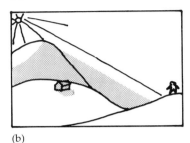

(b)

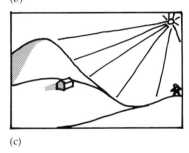

(c)

Lighting direction:
(a) side light;
(b) back light;
(c) front light.

adequate and more appropriate in areas subjected to softer, muted light such as Scotland or Ireland, whereas strong, bright colours suit Mediterranean or tropical lands such as Spain or Greece, Brazil or India (see Colour).

The lighting direction is the other important variable influencing how we see the landscape.

In side-lit conditions a scene is illuminated from one side relative to the viewer's position. Shadows tend to be cast which show up the three-dimensional relief of any landform (Plate 16). The lit areas show surface detail. East- or west-facing surfaces such as hillsides tend to be side-lit at particular times of day. Some landforms are especially effectively displayed under side-lit conditions.

When a landscape is back-lit the viewer is looking into the direction of the sun and therefore on to the shady side of landform or objects (Plate 17). Skylines tend to stand out because of the increased contrast of sky and shadowed land. Surface detail is reduced. In high latitudes the low sun angle in winter causes back-lit conditions on some slopes which may be almost continuously in shadow throughout the whole season and thus seem to be gloomy and oppressive. In such circumstances the winter shade line must be checked when siting a building in order to avoid permanent shade for the whole winter. Planting trees on shady slopes, perhaps behind housing, may increase the shade as they grow and accentuate the sense of gloom during the winter. Conversely, in lower latitudes back-lit and shady slopes are cooler and to be preferred for dwellings in order to avoid the strongest effects of the sun.

Front-lit conditions occur when the sun is behind the viewer. Landform appears flattened since shadows are reduced, but surface detail stands out as it is more strongly illuminated (Plate 18). Some landscapes, for example south-facing slopes in the northern hemisphere, are usually front-lit for a large part of the day either side of noon when the sun is highest in the sky.

When the sun is very high in the sky or overhead, such as in low latitudes, the scene will be top-lit. Objects cast shadows beneath them and light penetrates through the crowns of trees as shafts into the darkness beneath. Roofs may seem a much lighter colour than the walls of buildings owing to their higher reflectivity.

The lighting direction and the amount of light falling on the landscape influence which parts of the landscape draw our attention when we look at them. When assessing the landscape, perhaps prior to design, it is preferable to record it under a range of different conditions. We must not forget that we can also respond emotionally to certain lighting conditions. The effect of sunlight amongst storm clouds (Plate 19), the splendour of a richly coloured sunset or the moonlight reflected on newly fallen snow may evoke a quickening pulse, a surge of joy or make us catch our breath. It may be that the drama of the lighting effect in such circumstances draws attention away from the true state of the landscape.

With artificial light we are able to achieve complete control over colour, strength and direction. Using it, our attention can be focused towards particular features, say the main elements of a building or bridge, and keep unsightly features in darkness. Some scenes, especially urban ones, look completely different in the cold light of day from the glamorous effect of the lights at night (Plate 20).

Visual force

- Sensations of movement are present in static images or objects.
- The position of elements and their shapes can suggest an illusion of visual movement or force.
- The action of visual forces can be contradictory or complementary.
- Visual forces are ever present in landforms – running down ridges and convexities and valleys and concavities.
- Shapes or lines superimposed on the landscape react with visual forces in the landform.
- Compatible shapes responding to visual force will produce a more resolved, unified result.

The phenomenon of visual force is an illusion or sensation of movement created by a static image, object or the juxtaposition of a number of elements in a composition or landscape. Strong visual forces are the basis of such optical illusions as the moiré effect where often visually disturbing images appear to pulsate, vibrate or cause straight lines to appear to bend.

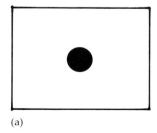
(a)

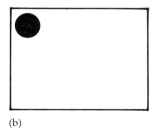
(b)

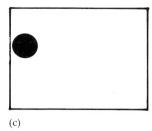
(c)

The position of an element begins to exert a force in relation to its surroundings:
  (a) the central position is stable;
  (b) the top position is unstable;
  (c) the point seems to be sliding down the edge of the plane.

Visual force

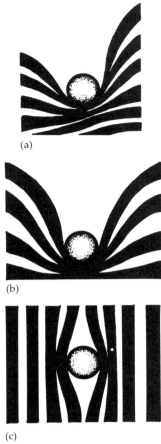

(a)

(b)

(c)

(d)

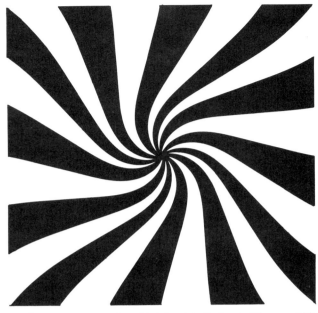

This pattern produces a strong sensation of twisting into the heart of the composition.

Visual forces operating in different ways:
(a) a sideways movement compressing the black stripes;
(b) a downward force stretching and compressing the stripes;
(c) the stripes being forced apart;
(d) movement cutting through the stripes – less responsive or harmonious compared with the other three examples.

The action of visual forces can seem contradictory or complementary. If they contradict each other or the apparent force of one element does not cause a reciprocal response in another then the unresolved tension which results can be severely disruptive and detract from a design (see Tension). The more an element responds to the visual forces of another in a complementary way, the more they are perceived as parts of an overall composition and greater visual unity results (see Unity).

Visual forces can be generated in several ways. The position of a point can create a visual force; so can shapes, especially if they have directional qualities. Arrows and chevrons on road signs are familiar and powerful examples of this. Lines can suggest movement which, when combined with direction, can produce different sensations of speed.

When we look at the landscape our eyes are constantly and subconsciously reacting to the visual forces present. They are led around a scene in a dynamic way, drawn by a whole range of features. Obvious lines such as a sinuous road or a meandering river invite us to follow them with our eyes; the contrast of bright sky with darker land attracts our attention. It has been widely observed that for many people the eye tends to be drawn down spurs, ridges and convex landforms and up into hollows, valleys and concave landforms. This holds true for all but the flattest landscapes. Normally a hierarchy exists so that it is possible to analyse a landscape in terms of strong visual forces flowing down

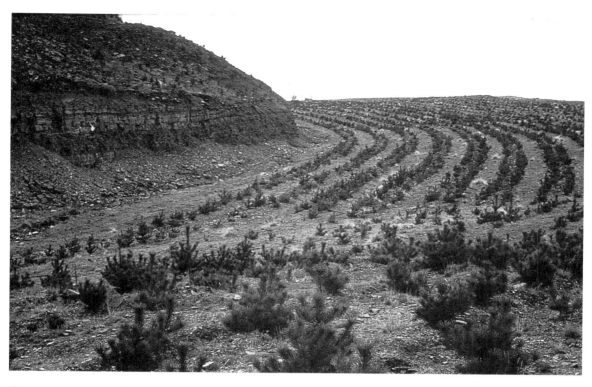

This rock outcrop appears to be pushing the rows of planted trees out and to the right.

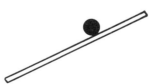

In this abstract the black circle seems to be rolling down the sloping line.

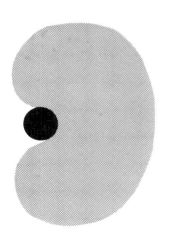

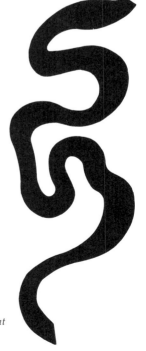

The black circle appears to be pushing into the grey mass.

A sinuous, meandering, flowing movement from top to bottom.

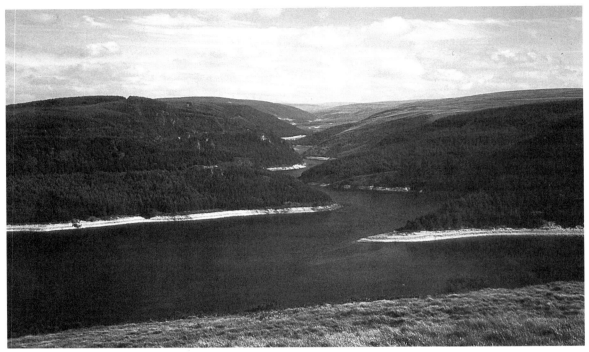

(a)

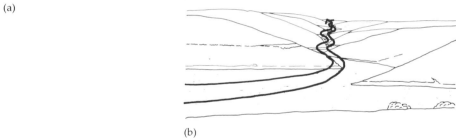

(b)

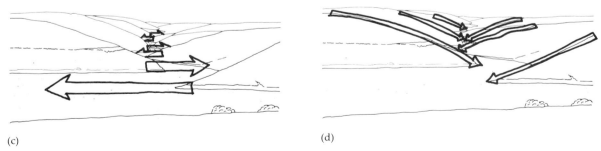

(c)   (d)

An analysis of visual forces operating in the landscape.
*   (a) Llyn Brianne, a reservoir nestling in the hills of South Wales.*
*   (b) The eye picks up the water and follows it into the heart of the composition.*
*   (c) A zig-zag movement is induced by the interlocking spurs.*
*   (d) We follow the line of the spurs down towards the water. They seem to be pushing inwards towards each other, squeezing the water area.*

prominent ridges or up deeper concavities, with lesser forces related to more minor features. This can also be seen at different scales or viewing distances.

These lines of visual force are powerful. Hence any plane or line superimposed on the landscape, whose shape, position, direction and own visual forces conflict with those of the underlying landform, will create unresolved tension which is likely to have a disruptive visual effect. This can be seen in the example of a road which cuts across a hillside in an insensitive way thus interrupting the skyline which naturally draws the eye. Another example is the shape of a square block of forest sitting uncomfortably on a hillside; this is more obvious because of the colour and texture contrast. Similarly, a rectangular clear cut in an extensive forest on mountainous terrain produces the same uncomfortable effects; it is a combination of shape and position conflicting with the lines of visual force in the landscape.

Once the way visual forces work is understood, it is possible to work with them. In landform, if a line or the edge of a shape such as a forest rises up into hollows following the upward forces and flows down on ridges with the downward forces a direct and compatible relationship between the line and the underlying landform will result. There will be no tension in the design which will be better unified.

An example of a semi-natural pattern related to the landform in a similar fashion to visual forces. Here the woodland is concentrated on the lower slopes and runs up the hollows while the open ground pushes down the spurs. The vegetation on the open hill responds in the same way, bracken rising up into the hollows while the grass and heather is concentrated on the ridges. These patterns occur due to a combination of management and physical factors.

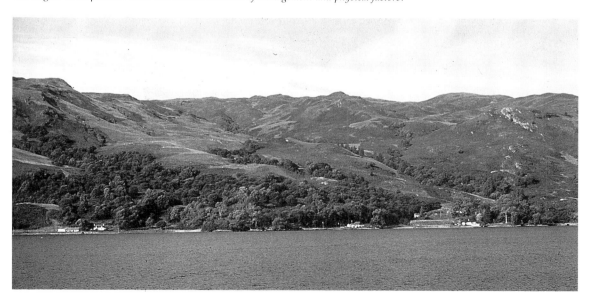

Visual inertia

- Certain objects may not show visual force: they may suggest inertness.
- Heavy, ultra-stable, horizontal forms seem most inert.

Although most forms exhibit visual force, it is possible for certain objects to appear more or less inert. This is usually a feature of solid volumes whose form and sometimes colour causes them to seem heavy, ground-hugging and extremely stable. A pyramid of shallow angle, a cube on a flat horizontal plane, a low dome or a

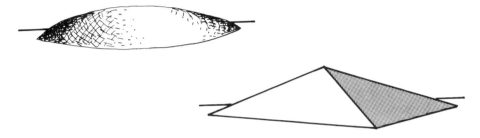

Two forms which are visually extremely stable and inert.

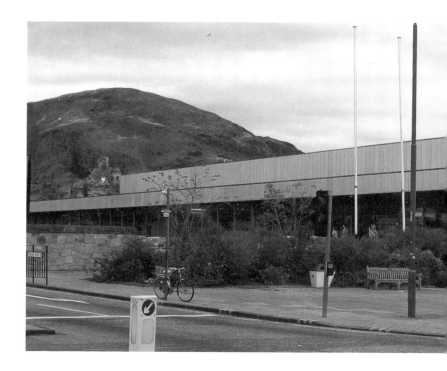

low, flat building are examples. Even then there may be minor visual forces running down the ridge lines of the form but the object itself still seems very inert requiring strong external visual forces to create any tension.

The need for inertia may arise in order to maintain a calm and quiet appearance in a composition or landscape to counteract visual energy and movement elsewhere. The use of a squat form and dark colour for a mundane and utilitarian building may help to avoid attention being drawn to it in a landscape of competing attractions.

A low, flat, predominantly horizontal building – visually inert in comparison to the surrounding buildings. Royal Commonwealth Pool, Edinburgh, Scotland.

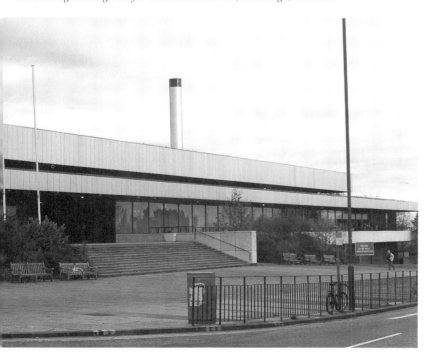

3

Organization

Objectives of design

Spatial cues

Structural elements

Ordering

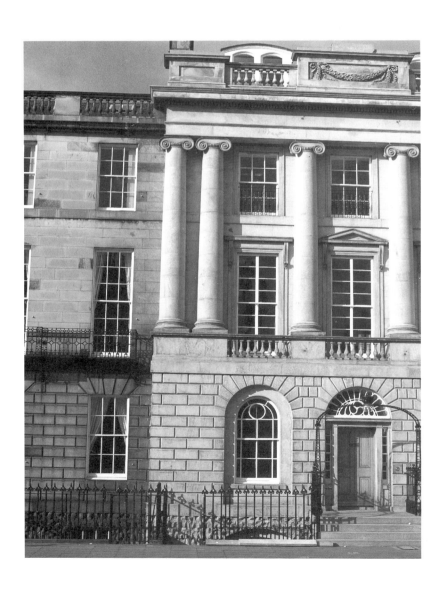

3

Organization

Inherent in the structure of the mind is the tendency to organize what we see. It is so strong that the slightest indication of possible connections are enough to cause the perception of a connected path or a complete form.

GARRETT, 1969

The ultimate visual objective in any design is to balance unity with diversity and to respect the spirit of the place. The patterns and structure of a design, composition or landscape result from the organization of the basic elements in their endless variations. Certain patterns so created seem harmonious and unified, others discordant and chaotic. It is necessary, therefore, to examine in some detail the concepts of *unity*, *diversity* and *genius loci* before looking at the various means by which elements can be organized in the design process. These organizational principles can be grouped into three categories:

Spatial: nearness, enclosure, interlock, continuity, similarity, figure and ground;

Structural: balance, tension, rhythm, proportion, scale;

Ordering: axis, symmetry, hierarchy, datum, transformation.

Objectives of design

Unity

- Unity is necessary for the parts of a design to relate to one another as a whole.
- Many of the organizational factors contribute to unity.
- A unified design should also be lively, incorporating rhythm and resolved tension.

- Complementary unity involves the deliberate use of opposites or contrasts which nevertheless relate to the whole.
- Natural landscapes are normally well unified within themselves since the visual patterns relate to natural processes.
- Careless introduction of man-made patterns can disrupt the unity inherent in natural landscapes.
- In existing urban landscapes new elements need to respond to the continuity and texture while being able to stand out – a fine balance to achieve.
- It is possible to use design to assert a degree of unity in an otherwise chaotic scene by using some of the organizational factors.

Unity concerns the relationship between parts of a design or landscape to the whole. The organizational principles to be described in this chapter can be applied in such a way that a unified or disunified design can result. If the design is too diverse and apparently lacking in visual structure it can also tend to appear disunified. While contrast is important for vitality and interest, too much will cause a loss of unity in the resulting visual confusion. Unity seeks a balance between many of the principles, in harmonious relationships between them: for example, when contrast in shape, colour or texture is balanced with continuity or similarity.

In terms of variables we have seen that as number increases, so the design becomes more complex requiring the spatial arrangement of elements to be more carefully considered. The fewer the number of elements the easier it is to unify the design. The position of one or more elements will have an effect – points can be arranged along a line (datum) and be tied together, they can occupy a similar position in space and be near each other. If each element contrasts too strongly these devices may emphasize disunity: therefore greater similarity in size, shape, texture and colour will ensure unity in a design. If similarity, balance, good scale and proportion are used inflexibly this may create rather lifeless harmonies in a composition. The careful inclusion of tension, rhythm and movement should not be overlooked as a means of adding life to a design without disrupting unity. The main consideration of organizational principles in this chapter will explore these aspects in detail.

If a design is to be truly creative, possessing an identifiable, if not unique character there must be some all-embracing, unifying theme, a sort of constant idea behind it. This might be a repeated motif, an invisible organizing grid, a mathematical formula describing the use of a material, or an abstract idea.

Without some of the contrasts or opposing characteristics of

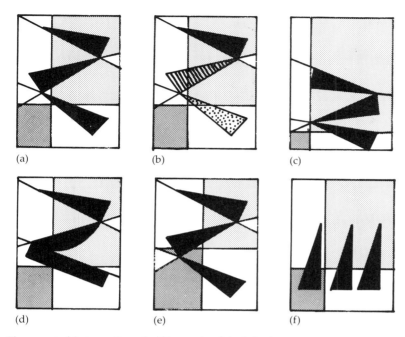

(a)   (b)   (c)

(d)   (e)   (f)

The concept of design unity explored in a series of six abstracts.
  (a) This design uses three repeated similar shapes set against a background divided into well-proportioned segments. There is rhythm and movement in the black shapes which are also tied into the composition by structural lines. This is a well-unified design.
  (b) In this example the design is the same as (a) except that each of the main shapes has a different texture. While shape is dominant, the extra diversity and contrast of textures together with the imbalance of visual weight reduces unity.
  (c) The division of the background and the position of the three black shapes is out of balance so unity has been lost.
  (d) The three shapes are dissimilar and this removes the sense of rhythm also, losing unity.
  (e) The background toned areas are split 50:50 so the proportions are lost as is balance, reducing the unity.
  (f) The positions of the black shapes have become static and lifeless. The composition is less interesting and unity is lost.

many of the variables a design may be difficult to perceive because it would have no background or context. To avoid this, mass should be set against space, light against darkness, movement against stability. As changes take place in the design or landscape over time, through the processes of growth or weathering, or through changing light conditions, this aspect should be kept in balance with the starting point and the original idea. This complementary unity achieved between opposites and set in a framework of change must be understood and used if designs are to be creative and dynamic rather than assembled according to a framework or rulebook.

Apart from fine art where the work of art may stand alone as in its own right with no immediate reference to its surroundings, it

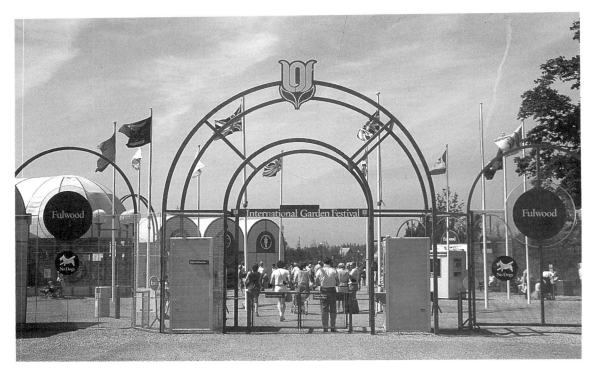

The use of repeated form and colour in a range of different elements has enabled unity to be established in this example from Liverpool International Garden Festival, Liverpool, England.

is usual for a building, a piece of landscape design or management activity to be seen in relation to its setting. A natural landscape undisturbed by man usually exhibits a great deal of unity. This is especially true of vegetation and drainage superimposed on landform where the resultant patterns are clearly related to each other at a range of scales.

An example of natural unity might be a pattern of forest on a mountainside. The trees will vary in species depending on soil, elevation, aspect and moisture. They will show a graduation of density. The shape of the margin of the forest to alpine areas above it will respond to other factors. In all of this there is likely to be a high degree of similarity of shapes, colours, texture and diversity; there will probably be rhythm and unity in the landscape. Since the patterns are unaffected by man the role of each part of the ecosystem in relation to the rest will have developed to reach some sort of equilibrium for the time and place. Continuity will be strong, giving a visual result which is harmonious, balanced and in scale with the landscape. Occasional unusual elements such as a band of hard rock may produce a point of contrast in the shape of a waterfall; perhaps volcanic activity will also add variety and dynamism to the landscape. This will add to the complementaty unity of the scene and also to the *genius loci*, the spirit of place.

Man-made patterns often introduce strong contrasts into a wild landscape: for instance, a straight line produced by a road or powerline, a field cut out of a forest, a quarry or mine on a mountainside. These can cause visual disruption not only because the contrasts they invoke are out of balance but also because they can be perceived to sully the wilderness. The forms of these elements may be incompatible, the colours and textures may clash or the position of some artefacts may cause visual tension.

Similar considerations can apply in a fine urban landscape where there is strong unity in the design of the buildings and the articulation of the urban space. The introduction of a new building in a modern style may contribute to complementary unity by drawing attention to itself and contrasting with its surroundings; but it will only be successful if it also manages to achieve a balance with the ingredients of its setting. There may need to be references to the surroundings brought out in the design, perhaps in the use of similar materials, shapes or colours. In other words, some aspect of continuity between the building and its surroundings needs to be expressed.

A pattern of natural elements well unified in the landscape. Here the forest area follows the landform, being related to drainage pattern. The location of shelter and soil, rock outcrops and climatic factors has resulted in the surface pattern being strongly related to landform. An analysis of visual forces would show that the forest is predominantly related to the valleys and hollows while the spurs are free of trees. The road line in the foreground stands out to some degree but also relates to the landform and so is reasonably well unified.

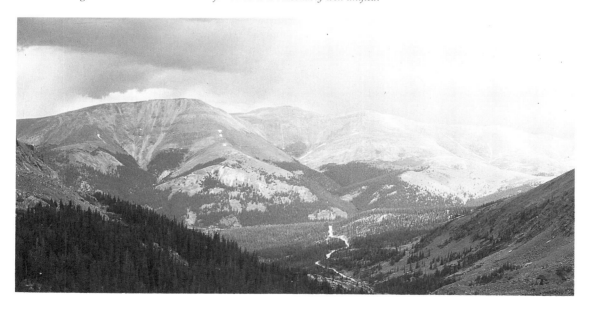

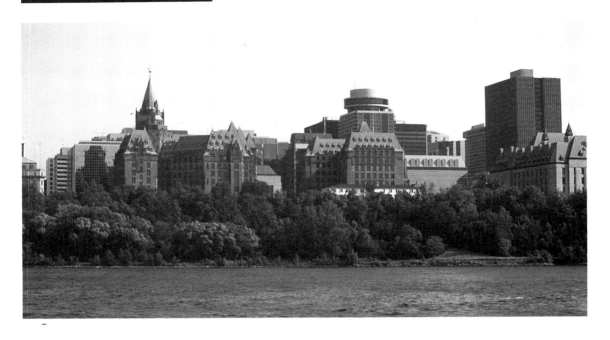

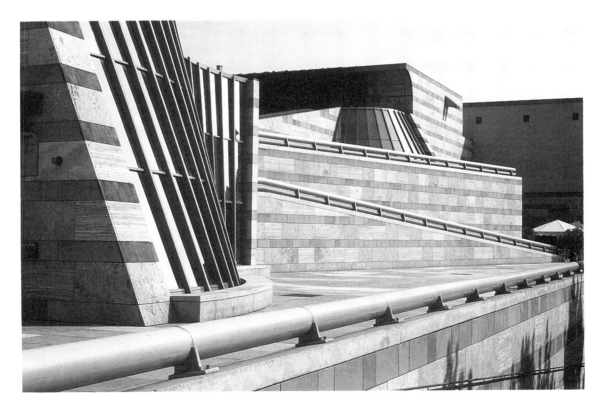

In many circumstances certain features stand out as dominant contributors to landscape character. The insertion of a new element into any landscape must take the dominant characteristic into account. For example, landform may provide the dominant influence, the visual forces generated being strong. Where the landform is rounded and flowing, a road which is laid out in a series of straight zig-zag sections does not respond and will therefore appear disunified. It may also disrupt the visual forces across the landscape and create unresolved tension.

In other settings there may be an opportunity to introduce unity into an existing confusing scene: for example, by superimposing a new pattern. The organization of a hierarchy, the provision of scale and balance may help to resolve the jumble. Where a group of buildings stand out as intrusive in their setting some way may be found of unifying them into their surroundings, perhaps by painting in compatible colours or by linking them into the landscape with other elements such as groups of trees.

A composition of similar architectural forms which shows a strong sense of unity. The repeated roof forms, window patterns and general proportions of the foreground buildings are similar enough to be strongly related. The background buildings are less well unified because of different form, scale and proportions but they are not dominant enough to reduce unity entirely. The presence of the woodland along the base acts as a datum to tie all the façades together visually. Houses of Parliament, Ottawa, Canada.

Diversity

- Diversity is concerned with variety in a design or landscape.
- Diversity is recognized as being valuable in many ways.
- Diversity varies in its scale from wide expanses of similar landscape to much more intricate variations over shorter distances.
- Increasing diversity tends to reduce scale.
- Areas of more hostile climate tend to have visually less diverse vegetation patterns.
- Longer-settled landscapes are usually more diverse than more recent ones because of the accumulated remains of human activity.
- Culturally mixed areas usually provide proportionately more diversity.
- Diversity must be balanced with unity – too much diversity can cause visual chaos.
- New elements in the landscape can increase or reduce diversity, depending on how they are treated.
- Landscapes where diversity occurs at a range of scales are the most satisfying.

A modern building, the Staatsgalerie in Stuttgart, Germany by James Stirling. This uses a bold composition of planes and lines. The repeated pattern of the windows and the strong lines of the handrails are offset by the simple, well-scaled texture of the cladding. There are some tensions present, as in the twisted plane of the window to the left, which are well resolved into the structure. The vertical lines on the windows have a rhythm which the eye can pick up from one to the other. The forms of each ramped terrace interlock with those of the window walls to integrate the overall composition further.

Diversity is concerned with the variety and differences in a design or landscape. It occurs at a range of scales and is necessary if a scene is to hold our interest for any length of time. It could be argued that there is a basic fundamental need for visual diversity in order to provide stimulus and enrichment to our quality of life.

Objectives of design

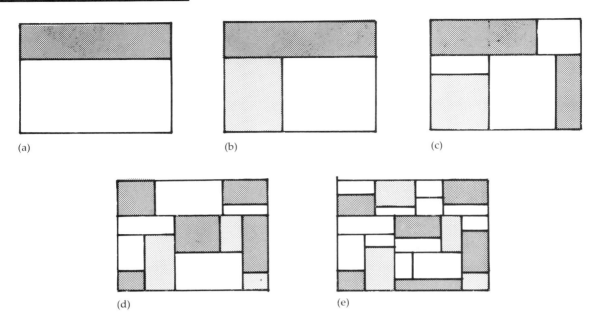

An abstract composition is subdivided to different degrees. From (a) to (d) the increasing diversity is more interesting. By (c) the degree of variety is becoming rather too much so that visual chaos is beginning to occur.

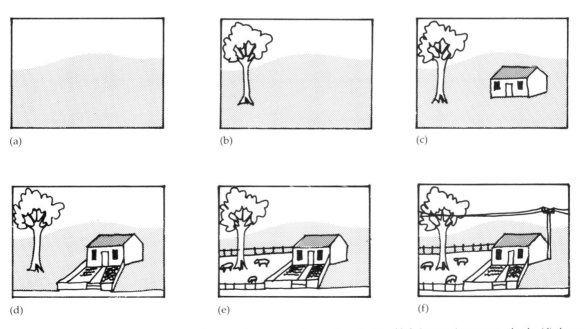

A scene where more and more elements are added. Interest increases so that by (d) the scene is quite varied. (e) is more varied still but retains some unity. By (f) the degree of diversity is too much and becomes disruptive.

This has been recognized by architects and landscape designers in the past, and more recently by psychologists. Early landscape designers such as Humphry Repton identified variety and intricacy as desirable attributes in their designs. This need may have arisen early in man's history through a recognition that landscapes containing variety tended to supply more food, opportunities for shelter and protection from predators as well as a greater chance of survival during climatic fluctuations or other periodic environmental stresses.

The degree of diversity found in the landscape depends on many factors. All natural life and man-made features and activities depend to a greater or lesser extent on the soils, geology and drainage of an area. Therefore, where there is a greater variety of rock types and landform a richer, more varied vegetation pattern usually results, giving greater scope for man's exploitation.

The relationship of visual diversity to underlying landform structures is reflected in the scale of diversity found in different places. For example, the Great Plains of North America are extensive areas with similar landform, soils, climate and natural vegetation which once contained huge herds of bison. The same types of agriculture such as grain farming or cattle ranching now occupy large tracts. It is possible to travel for several hours across certain states such as Wyoming or Nebraska and see little change in the overall appearance of the landscape. There are occasional details and subtle variation, but the overriding sensation is of monotony because the eye and brain quickly become fatigued looking at the same scene for long periods of time.

A long straight road across a featureless prairie in Idaho, USA. Here any diversity is on a very small scale so that it does not register as one drives across the area. The initial novelty soon wears off and the lack of interest can soon become boring. It is possible to drive across this type of landscape for several hours at a time.

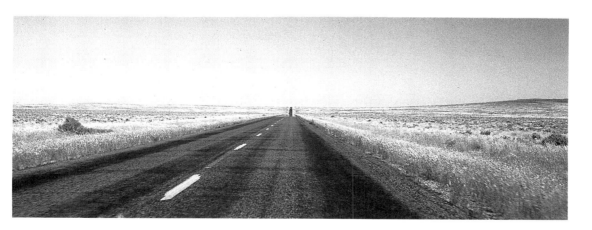

This can be contrasted with Britain where the geology varies considerably over much shorter distances. Here, in the space of a few hours a traveller can pass from the rolling, grass-covered chalk downland and wheat fields of Wiltshire into the limestone landscape of the Cotswolds and on to Herefordshire with half-timbered houses, small hedged fields and extensive trees and woodlands nestling amongst small hills. Part of this variety results from the long history of human settlement and the fine tuning of man's activities to the land over many centuries compared with the much more recent settlement of the plains states of the USA or Canada.

The degree of diversity in a landscape is also affected by the climate – the more hostile it is the simpler the pattern tends to be at all scales. That is, if cold, heat or dryness are extreme then apart from the landform and geology which may be variable, the vegetation patterns tend to be more restricted involving fewer species. The tundra, the boreal forest or the deserts tend to be similar in character over large areas. In the Tropics, where the conditions for plant growth are at their optimum, the scene from a distance can also seem very monotonous, as a sea of dark green, but within the tropical rainforest there is an astonishing variety of plant and animal life not found in the areas of extreme climate.

The variety and interest provided by human settlement over long periods of time are reflected in the landscape in many ways. The palimpsest of human history present in the countries of Europe, the Middle East, India and China, for example, contributes to the degree of diversity and the character found in the landscapes of those areas (see Continuity).

Diversity also emerges where different cultures meet. The various styles of buildings, gardens and culture in general brought to the USA by its immigrants from many countries have led to an incredible variety of scenes in the different ethnic areas of cities such as New York, Chicago or San Francisco. This can also unleash new forms of creative activity and visual expression which can further diversify the appearance of those cities.

In any design the degree of visual diversity must be balanced against the need for unity. There are a number of consequences which can arise as diversity increases. In a monotonous composition or landscape, interest can be added by introducing new elements or variables. As this progresses those elements of diversity begin to interact more and more requiring greater organization of the composition in order to maintain unity. Finally variety may become out of control and visual chaos results. This effect can be seen in the uncontrolled proliferation of buildings and signs found along many 'strips' in the USA. A huge range of styles compete with each other and together with

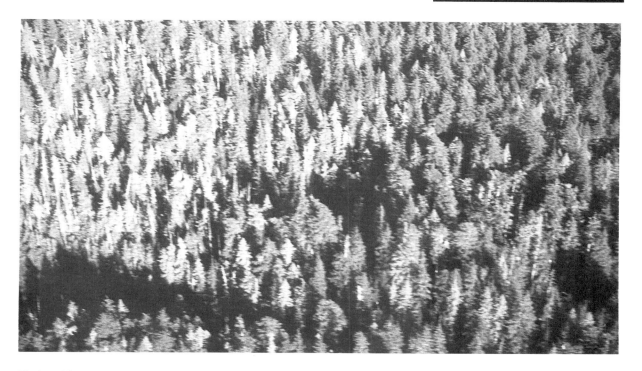

The boreal forest of northern British Columbia, Canada. This texture extends continuously for many thousands of square miles. In these climatically harsh areas the diversity at all scales is limited: even in the canopy there are few tree species and a limited range of plant and animal life compared with the tropics.

A 'strip' on the outskirts of a typical town in the USA. The wide scale of the highway and the simple plane of its surface is contrasted with the random scatter of buildings and signs which appears to be devoid of order or structure so that the result is visually chaotic. To make matters worse, each sign is trying to outdo the rest to attract the attention of drivers who are bombarded with a huge and confusing range of messages.

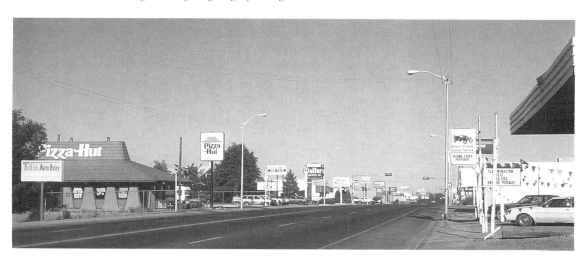

artefacts such as traffic lights and street lamps cause visual chaos. Only by bringing some discipline and organization into the design is this avoided.

There are effects on scale by increasing diversity. Large elements can be reduced in scale by being subdivided into different parts. In effect this is introducing diversity. Once again, the degree of diversity can become excessive, especially if there is no obvious hierarchy of scale, and unity can be lost. At the other extreme, the scale of the diversity can become so reduced that at a larger scale the effect can become monotonous. Humphry Repton recognized this when he applied the 'Rule of Thirds' to his landscape planting. He felt that balance, scale and unity could be maintained while diversity was satisfied if the planted area, a large group of trees for example, was dominated by one species occupying two thirds of the whole while the remaining one third could consist of a range of species (see Proportion).

When handling diversity in a newly created composition then a great deal can be controlled by the designer. However, inserting new elements into an existing landscape can have several consequences. If the existing landscape already contains a satis-factory amount of diversity the new element might tip the balance and add too much for unity to be maintained. Conversely it might reduce diversity and create a less interesting design.

An example of new elements causing too much diversity can be found in the case of a golf course laid out in a parkland landscape. The original layout would have been carefully de-signed to balance the masses of trees and to harmonize diversity with unity. The visual paraphernalia of a golf course – greens, fairways, bunkers, small groups of trees, flags and so on – adds a further degree of diversity at a small scale and can seriously disturb the balance of the original design.

The problem of reduced diversity can be found in parts of the south of England where hedgerows and trees have been removed or else lost owing to Dutch Elm Disease over the last 30 years. The former rich, highly diverse yet strongly unified landscape of small fields interspersed with trees has been replaced with a large-scale monotonous landscape of large green fields.

If not handled sensitively the diversity of the semi-natural vegetation patterns of the Scottish Highlands can be replaced or reduced by forestry plantations of a single species of tree. As long as the degree of diversity found in the existing landscape is reflected in the new forest design, such as in species variety and open areas left unplanted, then the overall unity of the landscape will be retained as will the visual interest of the scene.

In the same way one of the visual results of logging in natural forests in the USA and Canada has been to reduce scale and impose a highly diverse pattern of small units on a large-scale landscape which originally was lacking in diversity. It is ironic that many people see smaller felling areas as the answer to reducing their visual impact, whereas this reduces scale still further and increases visual chaos unless structural devices such as grouping the felling areas are adopted to prevent scale problems occurring (see Number, Nearness).

There is an interesting relationship between visual and ecological diversity. We have already seen that one of the most diverse landscapes ecologically is the tropical rainforest, yet seen from the air it can be extremely monotonous. Equally, a highly visually diverse landscape, particularly an urban one, may lack diversity ecologically. In a purely natural landscape there is likely to be a close relationship between the two at certain scales. Where there is some variation in, say, elevation or in a change from water to land, the plant communities will change and form patterns which are commensurate with the changes in the growing medium. This will be reflected in the level of visual diversity at the 'landscape' scale. One reason why we find certain landscapes more attractive than others may be this correlation of visual and ecological diversity, as seen in mountain areas or close to water.

As well as static elements in the landscape, much vitality and interest come from the presence of animals, birds and people. A structurally diverse, unified landscape is incomplete without them.

The weather, changing light conditions, cloud patterns and the wind further enliven and add ephemeral variety to the scene. The monotony of the prairies has been mentioned, but the sight of an electrical storm, a tornado or massed cloud formations compensates to some extent for the lack of interest at ground level.

In its most refined expression, diversity can reflect several scales. In an example such as Powys Castle in Mid Wales there is diversity within different parts of the landscape. The formal gardens are highly organized yet diverse in the range of plants, their form, colour and texture, and the artefacts present. The designed parkland contains diversity of mass, open space, tree forms and grass colour and texture. The enclosed agricultural land beyond the parkland demonstrates variety in the field colours, hedges and trees, again in a well-unified way. From the farmland the eye is led out to the mountains where diversity is provided by the semi-natural vegetation pattern. When looked at as a whole the entire scene contains diversity between the different parts of the landscape as well as within them. Moreover, each part of the landscape occupies a niche arranged within a hierarchy and in many ways suited in function and design to its location and by the qualities of soil and climate.

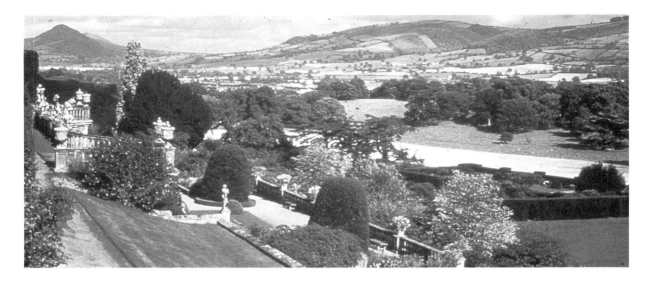

Powys Castle, Wales. In the foreground are formal gardens which give way to parkland, then enclosed fields and finally moor or woodland. This scale of diversity is particularly satisfying to behold. (Courtesy of Landscape Institute.)

Genius loci

- The *genius loci* or the spirit of the place refers to the special, unique quality one place has over another.
- *Genius loci* is intangible but is a highly valued aspect when attached to a landscape which helps to make it sensitive.
- *Genius loci* can be vulnerable because the factors contributing to it may be difficult to identify.
- Relatively extensive yet self-contained areas can possess *genius loci* as well as smaller-scale places.
- Any design must respond to a strong *genius loci*.
- A landscape lacking character can be given a stronger sense of place by good design creatively applied.

Genius loci, or the spirit of the place, is that quality or characteristic which makes one location of landscape different from any other, and that is unique and individual. The concept is somewhat abstract and intangible and tends to be more commonly understood on an emotional and subconscious level. It is, however, a most important attribute in a place and may be fragile and vulnerable when changes take place in or around the particular location.

Several people have written about the subject, most recently C. Norberg Schulz (1980) in his book *Genius Loci*. Place is very important to us and in our lives. Our sense of identity may be bound up with a particular place and we may refer to ourselves by this, for example, 'I am a Parisian'. The location itself marks the position of the place, but place itself consists of the totality of the natural and man-made things, assembled in a unique way and may well include the history and associations attached to the place by the people who identify with it. While all places have a character, this in itself is not adequate to induce *genius loci*. It is the uniqueness which makes it special and with which we can readily associate.

One of the difficult aspects of *genius loci* is that we may instantly sense its presence but be unable to identify what has created it. That is why it can be so vulnerable. Often the essence of *genius loci* can be teased out by an artist or writer who understands it in an emotive, often very personal way, yet also in a way which is accessible for the less sensitive or articulate. Landscape painters such as J.W.M. Turner or writers such as Thomas Hardy were particularly good at this.

Spruce Tree House, Mesa Verde, Colorado, USA. This is one of the many examples of Anasazi cliff dwellings which are hidden away in the bottom or on the sides of the canyons. The stone-built houses are clustered for shelter beneath the overhanging cliffs. It is almost possible to feel the presence of the former inhabitants who moved out leaving a hint of their culture behind. The sense of genius loci *is very strong.*

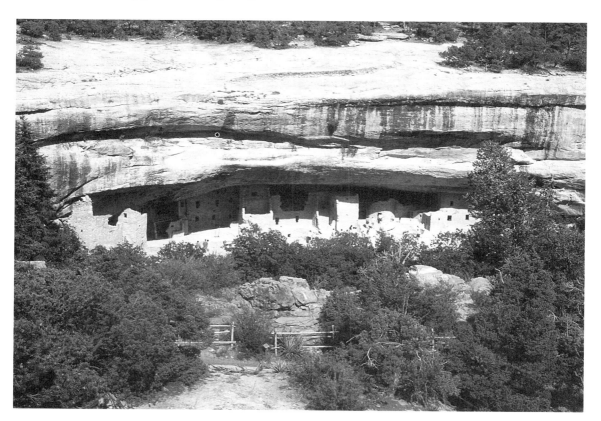

The spirit of place can be attached to relatively extensive areas. Mesa Verde National Park in Colorado is a prime example of a unique landscape distinct from its surroundings, made more mysterious by having been difficult of access and containing the remains of a little-understood people hidden in the depths of canyons within the Mesa. The landscape of the Mesa itself is distinctive. It consists of a flat-topped plateau covered in largely undisturbed vegetation and dissected by many ravines whose overhanging cliffs contain the *pueblos*, the stone-built dwellings of a native people known as the Anasazi (the 'Ancient Ones'). Here the sense of contact with people of times long past yet somehow close at hand is overwhelming. The dramatic visual context, the historical associations, the artefacts left behind by the people all combine to create a *genius loci* which anyone who visits the site should instantly recognize.

More intimate, smaller-scale places may also have strong *genius loci*. Hidden, secret places, dramatic features, particular combinations of natural forms, vegetation, water, light and landform can all be strong contributors. Natural places apparently untouched by man, such as a waterfall cascading into a canyon or ravine upon which we stumble by accident can affect us deeply. The drama of the falls, the thunderous noise of the water crashing over the rocks and reverberating around the ravine, the rainbow of light caught in the spray and the vegetation clinging to the cliffs may cause our hearts to leap and fill us with uplifting emotions which may persist long afterwards. The poet Wordsworth was deeply moved by the sight of daffodils in flower along the shores of a lake. The emotions came back to him:

> When oft upon my couch I lie
> In vacant or in pensive mood
> They flash upon that inward eye
> Which is the bliss of solitude
> And then my heart with pleasure fills
> And dances with the daffodils.

By applying all the design principles explained so far we can create well-unified and diverse landscapes. These may appear somewhat bland and even uninteresting unless each place is given its own individual character. Where the spirit of place is most obvious then the designer working in such a place must exercise very great care. This is because *genius loci* is an elusive quality which tends to be easier to conserve than create. It is certainly vulnerable to damage or destruction if not recognized or valued and treated with sufficient sensitivity. People tend to be more attached to a landscape with a strong sense of place and so are more likely to be sensitive to and wary of landscape change. An essential part of the analysis of any landscape should be to try to identify the *genius loci*. References to portrayals of a landscape in art and literature can be very helpful in this respect. By way of illustrating how vulnerable *genius loci* can be it is worth exploring the following examples.

The Montmorency Falls are to be found a few miles outside Quebec City in Canada. Here there is a dramatic waterfall which crashes over a precipice in one tremendous mass and churns up the water in the plunge pool below, generating much spray and mist. The water makes a deafening roar which echoes around the cliffs. Understandably the falls are very attractive to visitors. However, to reach the falls and to experience the full effect visitors firstly have to park their cars in an ugly parking lot on the side of a busy, noisy road. Then they have to walk through an underpass beneath a railway line. Beyond this the scene is one of electrical wires, a toilet block and a clutter of signs before the path leads on and around a corner to reveal the view of the falls themselves. In this way, because of the ill-considered development and visitor facilities, the spirit of place is severely compromised and the full effect of the falls is lost.

At another set of falls, Niagara Falls, the same sort of pressures apply, only this time wholly due to the huge numbers of visitors. In this case the falls are very large and less vulnerable in

A view of the approach to Montmorency Falls, Quebec, Canada. This is the kind of landscape a visitor has to pass through before reaching the falls.

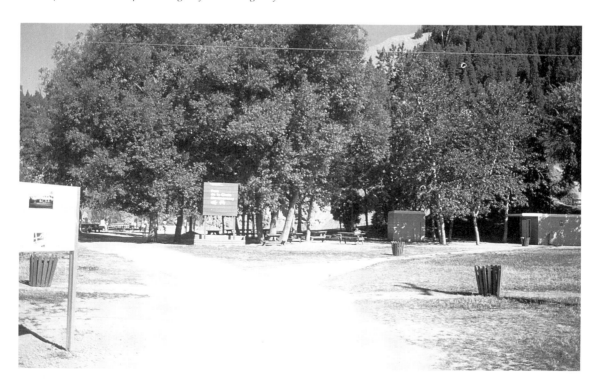

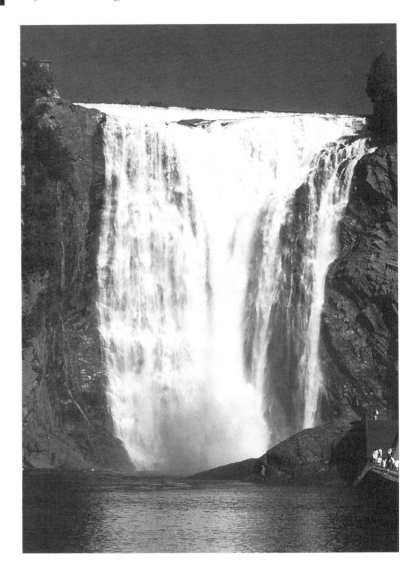

Montmorency Falls, Quebec, Canada. The scale, volume, water and noise are worth going to see but it is difficult to forget the clutter of the approach – which must be negotiated on the return to the car park.

themselves through the visitor-related development is in some danger of competing with and reducing the naturalness of the setting from which the falls are viewed. To some degree this has been controlled since the 1880s by the creation of a park (designed by F. Law Olmsted) between the river bank and the bluffs above the river upon which most of the town of Niagara Falls is built. This park has been laid out as a series of formal gardens but at least they ensure that it is possible to obtain a view of the falls where the sight of man-made objects has been reduced to a minimum. One exception to this is the presence of the *Maid of the*

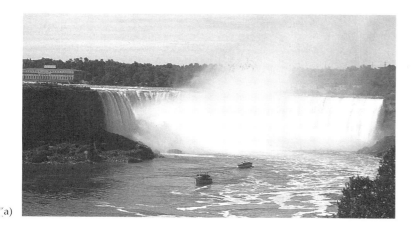

(a)

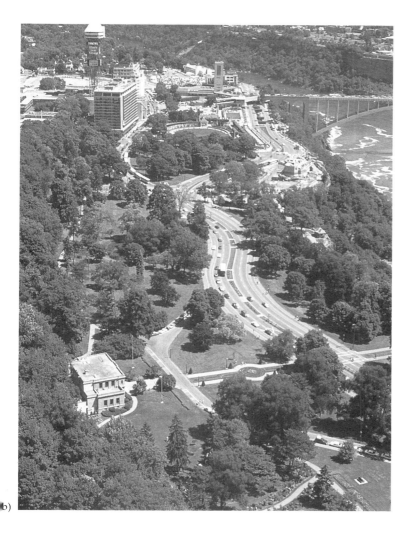

(b)

(a) The Horseshoe Falls at Niagara Falls, Ontario, Canada. The setting of the falls is reasonably well controlled. The falls are dominant and their power is emphasized by the small, vulnerable boats sailing into the spray.
(b) A view of the park at the falls. The town is restricted to the lower area and top of the bluffs. Below is a parkway set well back from the edge. The park layout is somewhat formal but the woodland on all the steep slopes provides a simple backdrop to the falls from most directions.

111

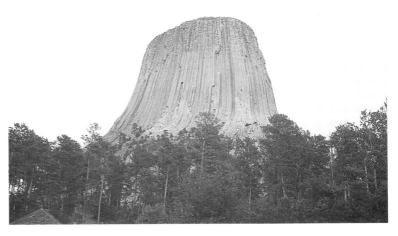

Devil's Tower National Monument,
Wyoming, USA. A dramatic solid volume,
the eroded remains of a volcanic plug,
stands out in the prairies. The genius loci
is strong, reinforced by the value attached to
it by native Indians who thought it was the
base of a giant tree scratched by a giant
bear.

Mist boats which take visitors close to the foot of the falls. Seeing these helps to give scale to the falls and serves to emphasize their size and power and enhances the sight of them.

When locating large elements or initiating management into a landscape, especially a predominantly natural one, there may be certain key elements which dominate or are particularly significant. Landform may be important, perhaps sculptural or otherwise special. The quality of this might be affected by, for example, afforestation which can blanket and hide the landform unless designed well to reflect it. Another route might be to identify those parts of the landscape which have less significance and where landscape change can be undertaken without detriment to the main factors influencing the *genius loci*. Logging in a natural, untouched forest in such circumstances may equally damage *genius loci* if it means that the quality of pristine wilderness will be lost.

So far we have considered examples where *genius loci* is strong and should be conserved during design. There may be others where it is weak or absent and where it can be created by design. This may be the case in a landscape dominated by the man-made, such as an area of urban development which has grown *ad hoc*. Here a strong creative contribution to overlay a new and appropriate character can help enormously.

An example of urban renewal which has restored *genius loci* can be found at the Inner Harbour at Baltimore, Maryland, USA. The area was revitalized in the early 1980s, one of the first such derelict sites to be tackled in this way. The area was redeveloped with a marina, shops, restaurants and outdoor plazas following the water's edge close to downtown Baltimore. The use of sculpture, the presence of old ships (the 1797 frigate *Constellation* and the *Chesapeake*) and the view across the harbour to Fort

Henry, prominent in the War of 1812 help to provide a local and historical character unique to the place. When enlivened by activities on- and off-shore the place becomes lively and vibrant. Altogether, it now has a strong sense of place. Criticism might be levelled at certain aspects such as the rather dominant tower block located close to the moored frigate and other places where the diversity of artefacts is excessive, but generally it all works very well.

Other examples of strong *genius loci* can be found in the landscapes associated with great country houses where conscious design transformed ordinary farmland into often magical landscapes modelled on the idealized classical scenes depicted in the paintings of Claude Lorraine, Salvator Rosa and Nicholas Poussin. Adorned with temples and statues and designed to ensure

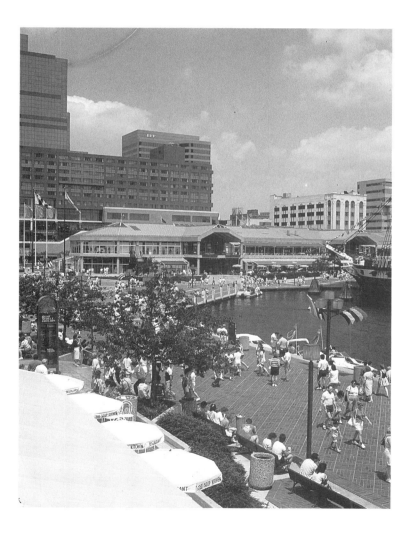

The Inner Harbour, Baltimore, Maryland, USA. This view shows the new esplanade, shops and cafes and the number of people enjoying the sunshine. Downtown Baltimore provides the backdrop and Fort Henry can be seen from the promenade itself.

that all views were contained within the idealized landscape, these represent one of the golden ages of landscape design and form part of a unified whole with the music, architecture and way of life of the aristocracy of eighteenth century England. This *genius loci* remains strong at places such as Castle Howard or Stourhead.

Spatial cues

This first grouping of organizing principles are all concerned with the relative positions of and interactions between elements in space. The principles are related to one another and normally a combination of them is present at any one time with one being the more dominant.

Nearness

- The closer elements are together the more we see them as a group.
- Closely spaced dissimilar elements may appear chaotic.
- Settlement patterns can vary depending on how near the houses are to each other.
- Trees and woods in the landscape often need to be near each other to have a structure at the correct scale.

The nearer visual elements are positioned together the more we tend to see them as a group. If the elements are very different, for example, in size, shape, colour then chaotic effects may result. Conversely, if a number of small, scattered objects are clustered together then the overall scale of the pattern may be improved and the overall effect appear less visually chaotic. The effect of nearness can be seen in many circumstances.

The character of a landscape where the settlements consist of houses spread out over a wide area can appear random and lacking in a clear pattern, whereas a nucleated settlement may look more ordered and clearer to understand. This can be seen in

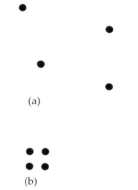

(a) Four points in space . . .
(b) . . . which together form a cluster.

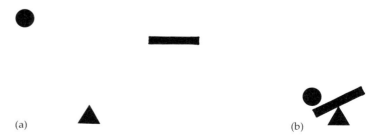

(a) These shapes are separate and do not read together.
(b) When located close to each other they seem to belong to a group.

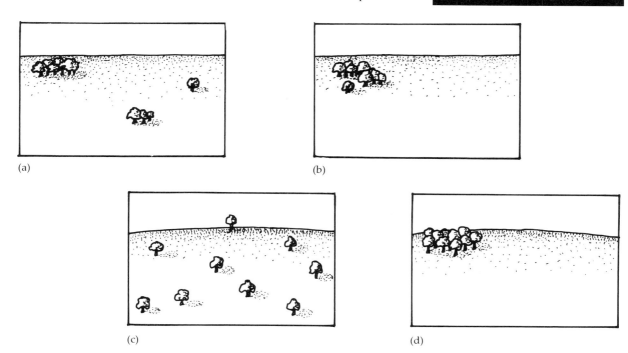

(a) Three clumps of trees in an open space . . .
(b) . . . achieve a better scale when located nearer each other.
(c) A scatter of trees . . .
(d) . . . has a better-defined entity when positioned closer together.

some areas of Ireland or the Western Isles of Scotland where houses are traditionally spread over the whole landscape because of the traditional tenure systems, such as crofting where small amounts of cultivable land adjoin the croft buildings. Compare this with country areas of England where strongly nucleated villages clearly separated from each other have their origins in the medieval feudal system.

The scale of the land-use pattern in the USA can mean that buildings, particularly in suburban areas, occupy relatively large plots for their size. This may be exacerbated by the large parking lots surrounding stores and restaurants on the out-of-town 'strips' which separate the buildings widely and prevent them reading as part of a group. A unifying pattern is therefore lacking resulting in a structureless appearance (see Diversity).

Trees may look better when planted in groups or at least near enough together to be seen as such in open landscapes. In much of southern England the Dutch Elm Disease removed a large part of the tree cover which until then had provided a strong structure to the landscape. The remaining trees and small woods often looked very forlorn because they were so far apart and looked lost

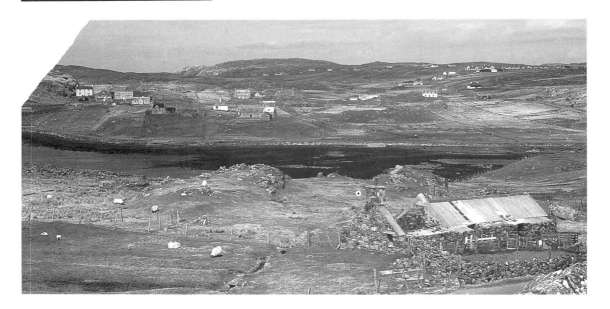

A dispersed settlement pattern on the Isle of Lewis in the Outer Hebrides, Scotland. Owing to the land tenure system of crofting where each cottage has its own area of land a scattered appearance results in this open landscape.

in the resulting open landscapes, where scale had increased dramatically owing to the loss of enclosure.

In forests the trees usually grow with their crowns coalescing together in order to optimize the site potential and to reduce competition. In order to maintain a forested appearance during felling or thinning sufficient numbers must be retained at close enough intervals that they are perceived as a continuous canopy. In orchards and olive groves the trees are not so dense as in a forest but they are still sufficiently closely spaced to form a pattern, seen as a texture at a distance.

Artefacts such as signs are often found together. When they do not conform to the same design, visual and functional confusion can occur. The more similar closely positioned elements of similar appearance are the more this confusion will be removed.

Enclosure

- When elements enclose space, both the elements and the space appear as complete forms.
- Enclosure is a function of the shape and position of elements.
- Completely enclosed spaces become inward-looking while partially enclosed spaces allow space to flow in and out.
- The fabric of urban landscapes may be perceived as a sequence of different sizes of enclosed space.
- Trees and small woods often depend on enclosed spaces to produce coherent patterns.
- Forests often provide complete enclosure which can produce oppressive, claustrophobic effects.

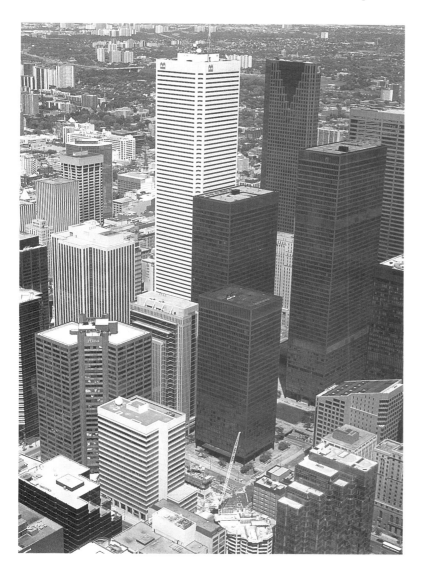

A mass of skyscrapers grouped together. When seen en masse like this there seems to be less of a dominant vertical emphasis although the scale effect seen from ground level is quite stupendous. Toronto viewed from the CN Tower, Canada.

These trees left after a heavy thinning in a small wood are not sufficiently close to each other to coalesce in the view and maintain an appearance of woodland.

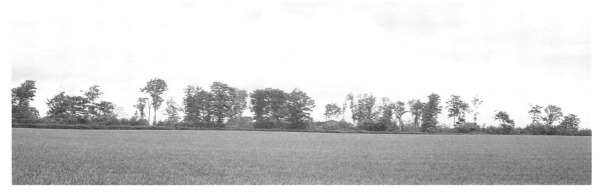

117

Spatial cues

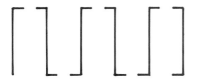

When the ends of lines are turned inwards they start to enclose space. As a result all size lines can be read as a single entity or form.

When elements suggest enclosed space we see both the elements and the space as a complete form. A series of parallel lines appears as a number of rectangles when the ends are bent inwards. Several parallel hedges partially enclose space and create open volumes in the same way.

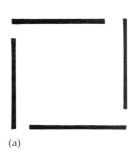

(a)

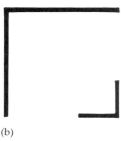

(b)

(a) Four lines positioned to enclose a space.
(b) The small element is strong enough to allow one's eyes to pick up the suggested shape and detect enclosure.

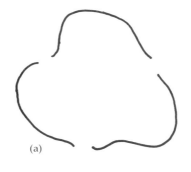

(a)

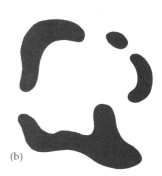

(b)

(a) Enclosure formed by irregular lines.
(b) Irregular planes create a similar degree of enclosure.

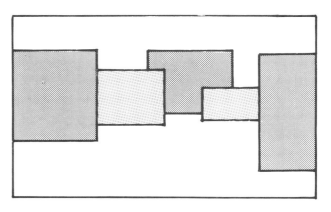

Enclosure created by overlapping vertical planes. These also coalesce together.

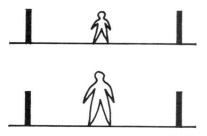

The degree of enclosure we perceive may depend on whether the enclosing element is above or below head height.

It is a combination of the shape of elements and their positions which creates enclosure. A single tree growing between two clumps may close the gap sufficiently to allow the eye to pass across it and visually separate one space from another.

The more complete the enclosed space is the more inward-looking the space becomes. Up to a point the enclosed or partially enclosed space retains a connection with the space outside and the two flow together (see Interlock). This balance of openness and enclosure can be manipulated in design to create different degrees of enclosed space in different parts of the design. An example of this could be in the hierarchy of spaces in a city enclosed by groups of buildings. As a person moves from space to space, from square to square, the different sizes of enclosure form a diverse but unified and structured pattern without monotony (see Hierarchy, Scale).

A landscape of trees, woods and hedgerows depends on enclosure for much of the coherence of the pattern. Shelterbelts are the most extreme examples of enclosing elements because they often produce complete enclosure and a sequence of separate inward-looking spaces. The effect of this can be to prevent any views out beyond the enclosed 'rooms' and to induce a feeling that the landscape is almost completely wooded, even though the actual amount of woodland and tree cover may be quite small. The heathland areas of Jutland in Denmark are a good example of this effect where the landscape is divided by shelterbelts which are only one tree wide. In other areas the pattern is much less regular with a wider variety of sizes of spaces and more chances for views through the landscape.

Two hedges at the Royal Botanic Gardens in Edinburgh, Scotland. In this example the ends of the hedges are partly turned in: a strong sense of enclosure is the result, clearly separating the foreground space from that beyond; yet the enclosure is not complete.

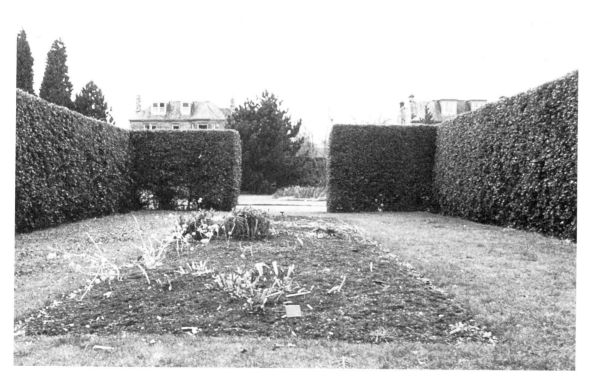

Spatial cues

A built example of enclosure: the space beyond the foreground opening seems more private than elsewhere, perhaps subconsciously belonging to the residents. London Docklands.

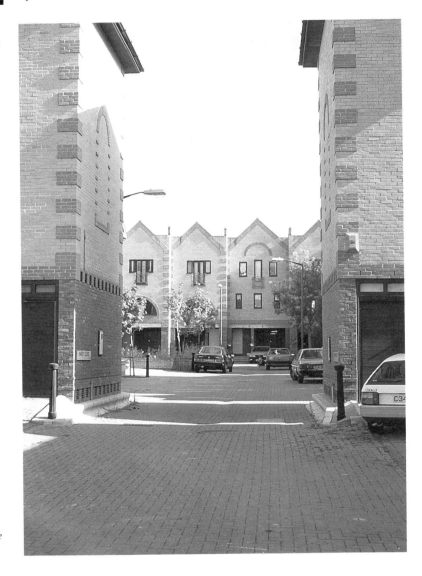

The vertical faces of these forest stands overlapping each other enclose the view. Smaller trees or a greater distance from the observer would not create as strong an effect.

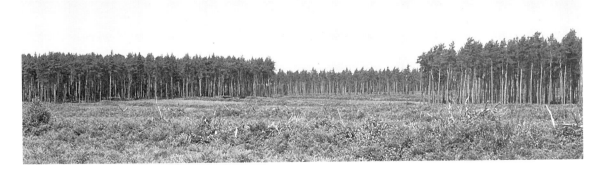

In forests the degree of enclosure partly depends on the effect of the tree trunks and their spacing, the height of the trees, their distance from the observer and the degree to which it is possible to see beneath the canopy. In forests the continuous enclosed feeling can be quite oppressive and claustrophobic for people used to more open landscapes.

In Britain the landscape is predominantly open and extensive views are possible in many places which balances any enclosed feelings present elsewhere. In large parts of Canada and the USA, where extensive forests still exist with dense undergrowth, the sense of closure dominates. When the forests completely clothe the tops of the hills and mountains, views are almost impossible to find and enclosure is complete.

Interlock

- Elements which interlock appear to become part of each other and more unified.
- Interlocking patterns are found in many natural or man-made landscapes.
- Buildings can be composed of numbers of interlocking forms.
- Groups of elements can produce an interlock of mass and space.
- The coalescence of elements positioned to overlap each other across space is another unifying device seen in the composition of building façades, woodland edges and rows of trees.

When elements interlock with each other they appear to become part of one another and thus form a more unified pattern. Planes which rest against each other are visually unconnected, whereas if they overlap, interpenetrate or enclose parts of each other, interlock occurs. A jigsaw puzzle is a simple example of two planes interlocking, as are patterns such as the Greek key.

Patterns of fields which have gradually been enclosed over many years may exhibit a more irregular interlocking pattern than ones which were laid out by surveyors at the time of the English Enclosure Acts. Vegetation patterns are usually quite strongly interlocked, a feature of shapes which have developed organically over time. Bracken, heather and grasses on a Scottish mountain side display this type of pattern as a result of soil, climate and man's influence. A great improvement can be made to the design of man-made forests if the patterns of tree species are not only organic in shape but also strongly interlocked.

Volumes can also interlock. Solid volumes such as the sections of a building can seem to push or interpenetrate into each other. Landforms also interlock: for example, a series of spurs along a winding river valley. When this is repeated then visual forces

Spatial cues

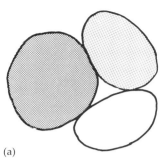

(a)

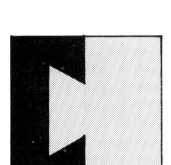

(a)

(b)

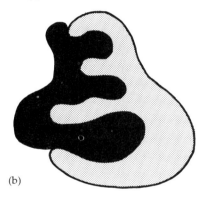

(b)

(a) Three planes which are not interlocked. They do not fit as comfortably together as . . .
(b) where, once interlocked they become part of one another.

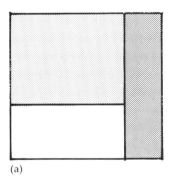

(a)

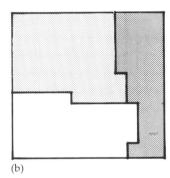

(b)

(a) Three rectangular planes laid next to each other . . .
(b) . . . interlocking, they connect together and become part of a unit.

(a) Two geometric planes interlocking like pieces of a jigsaw.
(b) Two organic shapes almost clasp each other in a strong embrace.

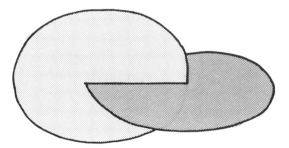

Two planes intersecting at right angles to one another.

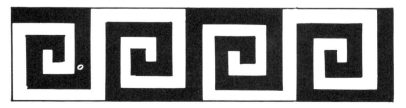

This is a version of the Greek key, an ancient pattern of interlocking shapes.

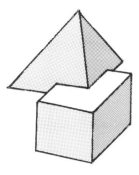 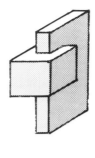

Two examples of interlocking geometric volumes.

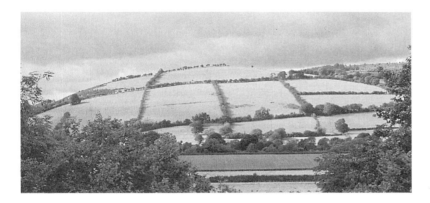

These fields do not interlock because the geometric pattern of the hedges is stronger.

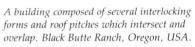

A building composed of several interlocking forms and roof pitches which intersect and overlap. Black Butte Ranch, Oregon, USA.

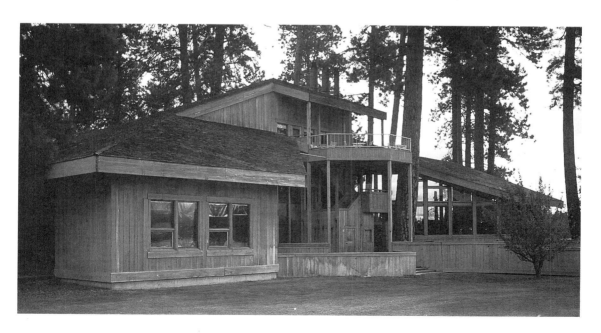

123

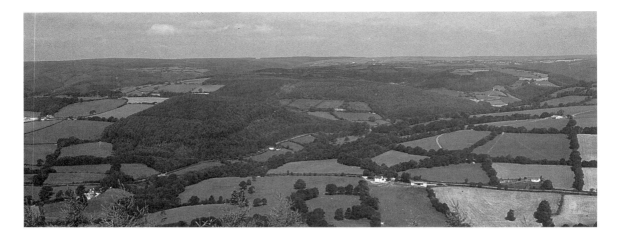

Woodland interlocking with a hedgerow field pattern which pushes into it and is partly enveloped by the woodland.

come into play and rhythms may be generated. Masses of woodland may interlock with open spaces to create open volumes which flow into one another. Interlock and enclosure combine to create a paticularly strong way of achieving a unified design. This is one of the main composing techniques used by the great eighteenth-century landscape gardeners, especially 'Capability' Brown.

As well as interlock with a horizontal emphasis there may be more vertical forms, such as overlapping planes of different heights. These may coalesce in the view and then react with the open space as before to give closure and interlock. Examples of these include the façades of buildings which are positioned so as to hide parts of each other, to enclose a space which flows in and out amongst them and leads the eye through the space. The edge of woodland, tall hedges or closely spaced rows of trees may also be used to define space using a combination of closure and interlock resulting in coalescence of the individual elements and a larger apparent size.

Continuity

- Patterns can show continuity in space, time or both.
- Growth stages in animals and plants show continuity of development connected to environmental conditions.
- Landscape patterns show continuity of extent, growth and development.
- Some patterns have developed gradually, others more quickly.

The presence of continuity of patterns in the landscape helps to control scale and to absorb small changes within a more dominant whole. Continuity can be spatial, when a pattern of elements

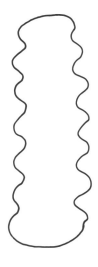
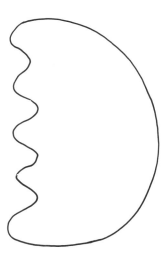

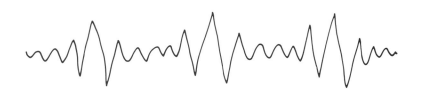

These lines represent continuity of movement and time – cyclical or linear but varied in frequency and intensity.

extends in two or three dimensions, or it can mean a continuity over time, such as the growth of plants or the cycles of the seasons. Interconnections between patterns at different scales also contribute to continuity. In many natural patterns the repetition of a particular shape at a range of sizes and scales represents an aspect of continuity which can be seen at a range of observer positions.

The predictability of patterns can be important: for example, knowing how a plant is going to grow and develop is necessary in design. The repetition of shapes and forms in a regular spatial arrangement as an organism grows can be seen in many ways. A mollusc such as a snail produces growth extensions on its shell each of which bears a mathematical relationship in size, angle and growth to each former one and to the conditions for growth. The resulting spiral form charts the history of the life of the animal (see Proportion).

A plant also grows according to a set of genetic rules varied by environmental conditions. The angle of each leaf to the stem, the arc between each successive leaf as they spiral around the stem, and the way branches occur combine with other factors such as soil and climate to create a certain pattern apparent in the plant as

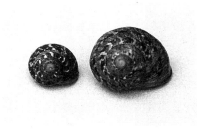

Snail shells: the spiral which increases in width as the animal grows represents a repetitive pattern determined genetically. The continuity of life and growth is repeated over time.

125

a whole and specific to it. The growth rings seen in a tree trunk also show its history. Wide rings stand for periods of fast growth, narrow ones slow growth, all as part of a continuous yet subtly changing pattern.

The spatial patterns in the landscape may grow and develop over time in an organic fashion leading to a strong sense of continuity. Settlements may have started in a small way and have gradually increased in size over many years. In Britain this development was originally not planned but slowly changing local traditions in building style, use of materials and methods of farming ensured that it took on a pattern which had continuity across large areas of similar landscape and over a long period of time.

Part of the prairie landscape of the USA. The continuity of the surveyed grid expands in all directions and imparts strong structure to the landscape.

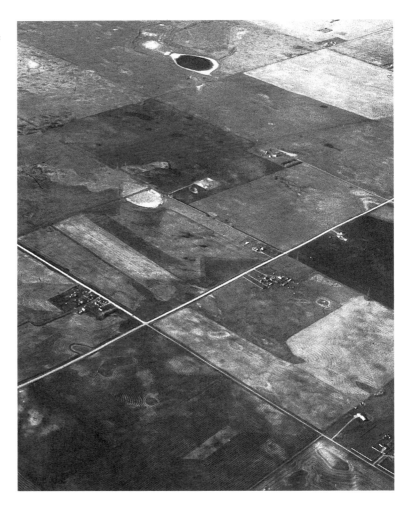

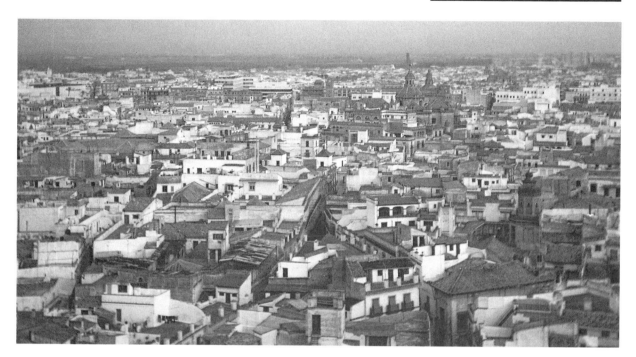

Planned landscapes such as agricultural areas enclosed by an Act of Parliament have another sense of continuity and another pattern. In countries which were recently colonized, such as the USA or Australia, these types of pattern have developed over a much shorter period of time. In the USA the surveyed Jeffersonian grid has ensured a very strong continuity in the pattern of settlements, agriculture and communication, local government boundaries and ownership. As different settlements have grown and expanded the denser pattern of built-up areas also has a strong sense of continuity about it.

While continuity on the scale described above is important its relentlessness can become monotonous unless one pattern is contrasted with another, or changes into another either in space or time. The contrast between a pattern of small fields which abruptly gives way to open hill or tightly packed, walled town located in a pattern of agriculture can be more interesting than a gradual transition of small to large fields culminating in open hill, or a town whose gradually reducing density of suburbs changes into fields. At a different scale, these contrasts may be seen as part of a wider pattern with its own sense of continuity (see Transformation).

Continuity over time is also important. For example, a forest may have existed since the Ice Ages or for even a much longer period in the case of tropical forests. The trees present today may be a few hundred years old or much younger but the forest itself

A pattern of urban fabric which has grown organically, each element (house, street) built and laid out according to custom so that a strong continuity in the pattern has resulted. Seville, Spain.

has continued as an ecosystem for the whole period. A managed forest may contain a wide variety of stands of trees of different ages and felling and regeneration may be happening continuously over the forest but this change occurs within a framework or pattern which continues over a much longer period. Thus continuity may provide a dynamic theme of stability at one level within which process and change can occur. Crops may change annually within an agricultural pattern yet the landscape never really changes. The individual buildings in a city are continuously being demolished and rebuilt yet the city remains.

Continuity represents the durable, long-term structures in the landscape allowing change to occur without chaos. As this process and change take place over a long period, we can begin to see which elements endure and take on a timeless quality and which are ephemeral and of little real, lasting value to us.

Similarity

- The more similar elements are the more we visually connect them.
- One variable can be more dominant allowing variation in others but still retaining similarity.
- Similarity of shape is a particularly dominant aspect.
- In nature, elements tend to be similar but not identical.

The more elements display similarity of shape, size, colour, texture and all the other variables the more we tend to connect them visually. Compatibility of shape, colour and texture are often key aspects creating unity in a design, or balance in a composition. The nearer together objects are in space the more we perceive them as a group. Hence the need for some degree of similarity to one another in order to achieve unity.

Often one variable can be more dominant allowing variation in

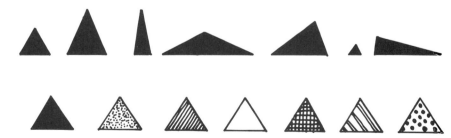

(a) These forms are all triangular but are not similar enough, in shape or size, to seem part of a family.
(b) The shape is the same although the pattern and texture of each triangle is different. However, the shape is more dominant so that they do read as a group.

Strong similarity of shape, size and texture ensures that these forms are read as part of a family group.

the others. Shape is a particularly dominant variable where the colour or texture, for example, can vary while the repeated form holds a design together. A pattern of fields can vary in colour while the field shapes are similar and maintain the cohesiveness of the design. There may be a hierarchy of shapes, with a strong geometric shape repeated which has lesser, more varied shapes within it (see Hierarchy, Scale). Alternatively, it may be the shape of part of a form or a unit of construction which is repeated in different ways. This could be a standard size and shape of a piece of timber used to construct a range of artefacts such as a fence, benches, tables or litter bins, or the size of a brick used in a house.

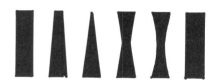

A group of shapes where there are some similarities and some differences – height, base width, colour are similar but shape is different to a greater or lesser extent.

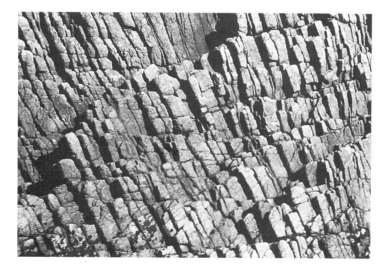

This rock face is composed of a number of units all similar in shape, size and colour although not identical. Because this is so the separate units become subsumed in an overall pattern.

When a shape or form is not so strong in its degree of similarity then other variables may be used. For instance, if a series of differently shaped buildings is reclad in the same coloured and textured material this may be enough to make them appear as part of a unified group. In combination, a limited range of a shape, a few colours, size of materials, method of construction and the way of positioning the final form may be used to give a 'family feel' to a set of, for example, signs or small buildings.

Some variables are weaker at creating unity through similarity. Position, orientation and interval, for instance, are not strong

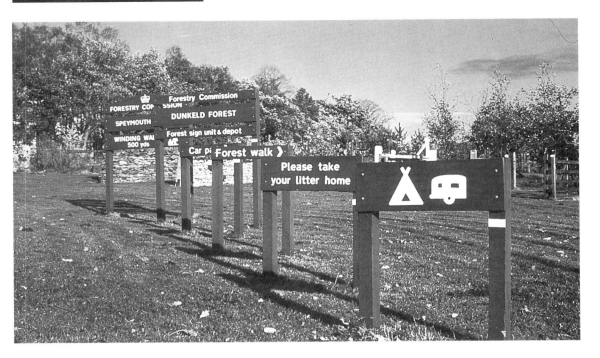

*A 'family' of signs. Each is constructed according to a system – size and shape of posts,
sizes of boards, typefaces for lettering and colours. Although the sizes vary as do the
numbers of individual elements in each sign the strong similarity dominates and each is
seen as part of the family.*

enough in themselves to override the dominance of shape or
colour.

It is important to recognize that in many ways it is more useful
in design to have similar elements than it is to have identical
ones. The latter can be monotonous and reduce diversity if used
too much and can look out of place in more natural landscapes
where similarity of form is more usual as no two trees or rocks are
ever identical. A balance has to be found which keeps interest
and character in a landscape while avoiding visual chaos.

Figure and ground

- Some forms or objects stand out as feataures or figures against a
  background.
- Figures are usually strongly contrásted with the ground.
- Sometimes what is figure and what is ground is ambiguous.
- Strong contrast can be a drawback in a design so reducing
  contrast can be used to avoid the figure standing out too much.
- Sometimes a figure needs to stand out for particular reasons.

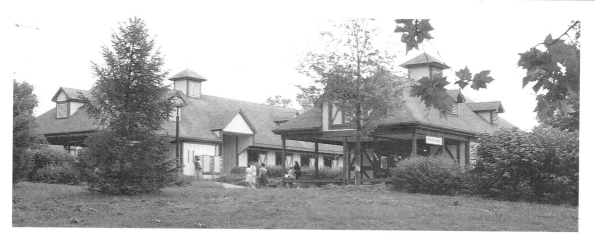

A series of buildings. The roof forms, textures and colour are repeated in similar ways on the porches and ventilators so that there is a subtle balance between sameness and variety which contributes to the interest of the composition. Kentucky Horse Park, USA.

In any design and in most landscapes some forms or objects stand out as features or figures against a more general background. Usually smaller objects, simple shapes, strong colours, dense forms, fine textures and solid volumes all tend to appear as figures. Examples include a person in an empty town square, a solitary house on a hillside, or a tall church standing out from the urban fabric of a tightly packed town.

Convex forms usually stand out as figures while concave ones appear as holes or voids. Any small mass in space is usually a figure. Occasionally the relationship is somewhat ambiguous, especially if there is little difference in size, if there is strong interlock or if the colours and textures are too similar. If the figure stands out too strongly from its surroundings and in so doing

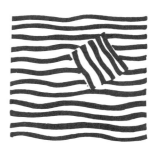

A section of texture turned to run the grain in a different direction is sufficient to produce a square figure showing against a background.

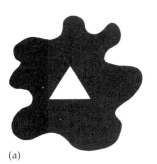

(a)

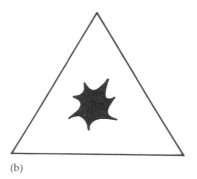

(b)

(a) The triangle stands out by contrast and its strong shape from the irregular plane which is the ground.
(b) The irregular shape appears as more of a void and the triangle remains as the figure.

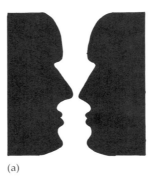
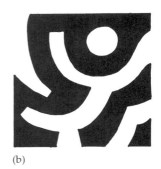

(a)   (b)

(a) Is it a vase or two faces looking at each other? This well-known example illustrates a balance – either can be figure or ground.
(b) In this strongly interlocked abstract it is difficult to tell what is figure and what is ground.

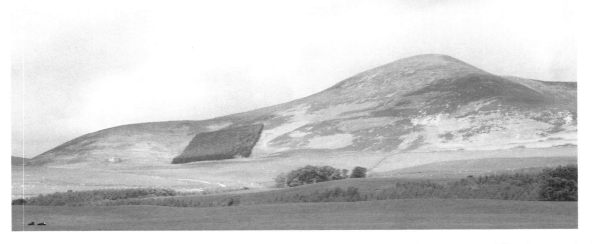

A square plantation of dark colour and fine texture stands out as a figure against the background of the hills. Midlothian, Scotland.

contrasts too much then it may be intrusive. This is a particularly common effect when geometric shapes are introduced into natural landscapes. Examples of this might be a building on a prairie, a car park in a forest or a clear cut area introduced into a forest. The intrusive effects can be mitigated by reducing any contrasts to a minimum in order to try to attach the form to its background and even to attempt to convert it from figure to ground. This can be achieved by the use of similarity in a carefully thought-out way.

There are plenty of cases in which it is desirable for figures to stand out from the background. Sculptures may consciously seek to emphasize the contrast of their form and material with that of their setting. Part of a design may depend on a strong focal point for its maximum effect such as an obelisk or folly. There may be

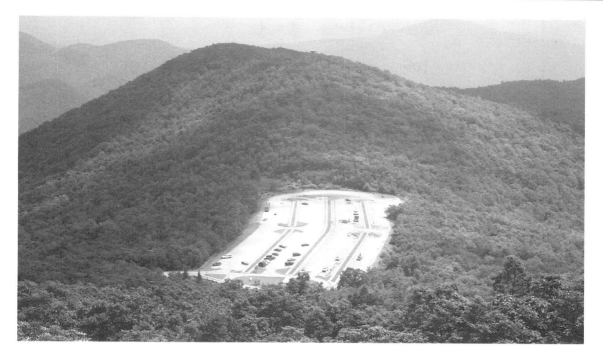

A car park with a reflective light-coloured surface stands out as a strong figure in the extensive background of forested hills in Chattahoochee National Forest, Georgia, USA.

symbolic reasons such as a church or temple standing out, or a large house or castle in order to remind people of who holds power (see Point, Position).

The basic rule regarding figure and ground can be summed up as follows: if the figure is important then it should stand out and the background should not compete with it; if the continuity of the texture and pattern of the background is important then individual elements should not stand out as figures.

Three important volumes – the church of Santa Croce, the Cathedral and the Medici Palace – rise as figures against the background of the roofs of Florence, Italy. These represent the symbolically important aspects of life when Florence was at its heyday in the Renaissance, so are visual manifestations of the power of the Medicis and the Catholic Church as well as demonstrations of the architectural prestige enjoyed by Florence at that time in the dome of the Cathedral.

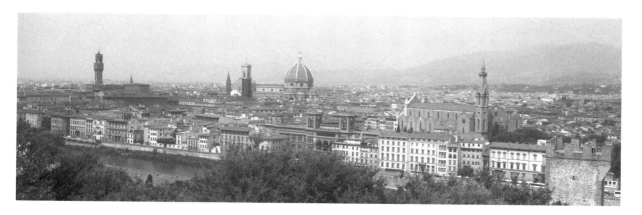

Structural elements

The next group of principles are structural: that is, they are concerned with the way the different parts of a design fit together and are related to each other.

Balance

- The equilibrium in a design or composition is affected by its visual energy.
- Factors affecting visual balance include direction, size, density, solidity, colour.
- Position has a very important effect on balance.
- There is a strong interrelationship between visual balance and symmetry.
- Balance in the landscape involves the relative amounts of different land uses.

The perceived state of equilibrium in a design or composition is affected by the action of visual energy present in the constituent parts. A balanced design is one where no further change is required in the interaction of the visual forces. Imbalance occurs

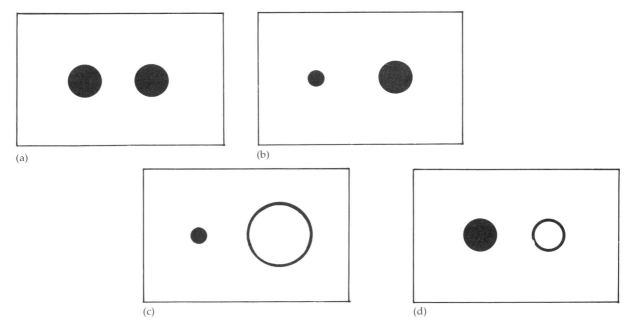

(a)

(b)

(c)

(d)

(a) Two circular planes balanced in terms of size, density and position.
(b) The composition is out of balance owing to the sizes being different.
(c) The sizes vary but the greater density of the smaller is balanced by the lower density of the larger.
(d) The variation in density means that although the elements are the same size they are unbalanced.

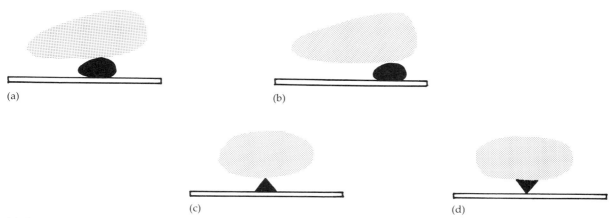

(a) This abstract looks balanced.
(b) The position of the black element means that the whole composition is top-heavy.
(c) This looks uneasy but balanced.
(d) This should be balanced but the inverted triangle causes it to look unbalanced.

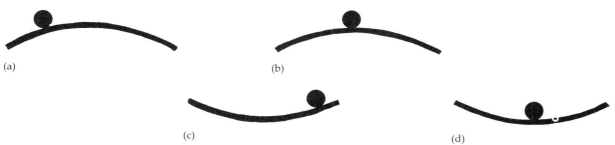

Balance and visual forces.
(a) The black point is unbalanced because it looks as if it is rolling off to the left.
(b) Here it is stable at the apex of the curve but strong visual forces want to pull it off.
(c) The point is rolling into the bottom of the curved line.
(d) The most stable position of all, where all visual forces are resolved.

when it is necessary to alter these forces by changing the elements in some way.

Several factors may affect balance. One of the most important is the direction of movement: for example, elements moving in opposite directions may balance one another. Another important factor is the apparent visual strength of the elements. Larger forms seem stronger than smaller ones, regular closed shapes are stronger than irregular open ones, and solid forms are stronger than diffuse ones. Similarly colour can affect visual strength – dark colours are stronger than light ones, advancing colours stronger than receding ones. Faster, longer and more frequent movement is stronger than slower, shorter and less frequent movement.

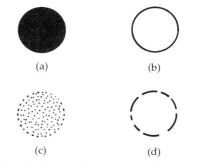

The visual strength of an object varies.
(a) Solid and dense forms are strongest.
(b) Open forms are less strong . . .
(c) . . . as are diffuse forms . . .
(d) . . . and least strong are open forms with indeterminate edges.

135

The position of forms has a strong effect on balance. Vertical positions are stronger than horizontal ones. The latter appear more stable as they are related to the horizontal line. Giving a horizontal emphasis to the roof of a building can be used to balance a series of vertical elements beneath.

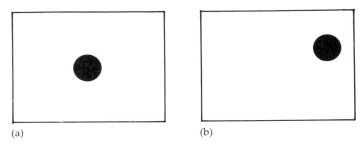

(a)   (b)

The position of these points affects the balance of the composition:
 (a) in the centre is complete equilibrium;
 (b) offset in the upper portion is unbalanced and visual forces are at play.

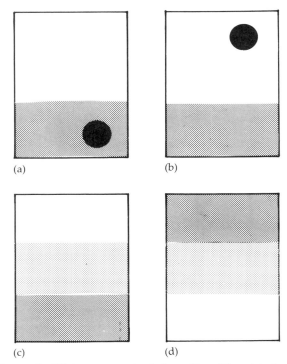

(a)   (b)

(c)   (d)

The visual strength of (b) is stronger owing to the position of the point whereas in (a) the point is not only at the bottom of the composition but is also within the toned area. The visual weight of (d) is greater than that of (c) owing to the denser parts being at the top of the form.

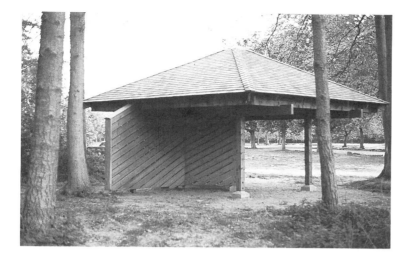

A small building which is physically balanced (i.e. it will not fall down) yet is visually unbalanced. This is because (a) the roof is top heavy for the size of the supporting uprights and (b) the diagonal boarding direction of the panelled area leads the eye in such a way that the building looks as though it should fall over to the right. Heavier uprights and a less dynamic panelling could restore balance.

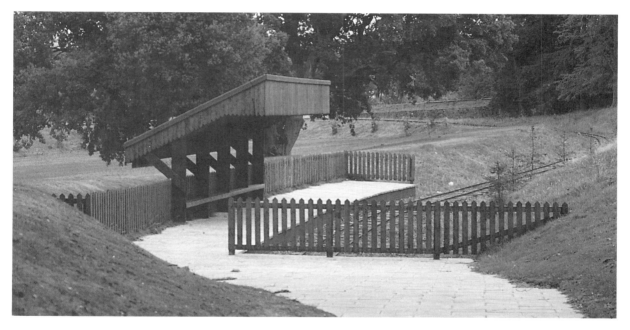

There is a strong relationship between balance and symmetry or asymmetry. Asymmetric balance can be used to create a freer, more adventurous and informal design while symmetry produces orderly, static and secure results (see Symmetry).

In the natural landscape balance often occurs asymmetrically. A large rock carried by a glacier may be left balanced on a smaller rock, a tree may grow leaning into the wind or an overhanging cliff may seem ready to fall down. These are all examples of real, physical forces being in equilibrium as opposed to purely visual forces although the result may be visually unbalanced.

Another small building, in which balance is resolved because the strong uprights and struts extending behind help to balance the otherwise visually strong canopy. The fence also adds visual weight to the lower part of the structure thus offsetting a tendency to be top-heavy.

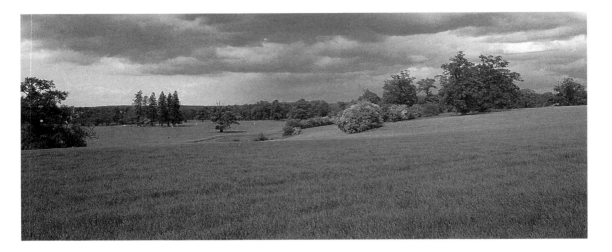

A parkland landscape composition which is well balanced in the proportion of open space and groups of trees. The groups of sequoias in the middle distance act as focal points and hold the eye. Hanbury Hall, Worcestershire, England.

In landscape design balance also involves the relative amounts of different land uses as seen from particular viewpoints, such as the relative proportions of woodland to open ground. Each land use produces its own visual strengths of colour, texture, shape and so on. These need to be balanced to prevent any one becoming too dominant (see Proportion and Scale).

A building may appear unbalanced because of the relative sizes of its constituent parts. The resulting visual energies and their relative positions make it look as though it is about to fall over. By understanding these factors balance can be restored or achieved and the visual forces given equilibrium.

A design can be balanced by the use of a small element of strong visual weight to offset a larger one of weaker visual weight. If the door of a building is painted a bright, strong colour such as red, this will balance the rest of the building if it is of a receding colour. A darker-coloured roof will have more visual weight and appear to hold down a building, thus assisting balance (see Colour).

Tension

- Tension occurs when visual forces conflict.
- Tension can increase the vitality of a design.
- Resolved tension can be dynamic yet harmonious.
- Lines responding to visual forces in the landscape display resolved tension.
- Visual tension may exist where physical tension is resolved.

Tension occurs as a result of conflicting visual forces. In some ways this can lead to imbalance but it can also increase the vitality of a design.

All forms exert visual forces to a greater or lesser degree. When these conflict or when a form exerting a strong force appears to be contradicted by a form exerting a weaker one, then tension will result. This is similar visually to the effect of a coiled spring restrained under physical tension; equilibrium or balance are only achieved once the tension has been released. This release can

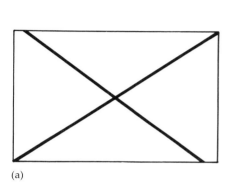 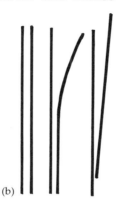

(a)   (b)

Two simple examples of visual tension.
   (a) One of the straight lines does not intersect the corners of the rectangle as we would expect it to.
   (b) All the lines should be parallel, yet some are pulling away.

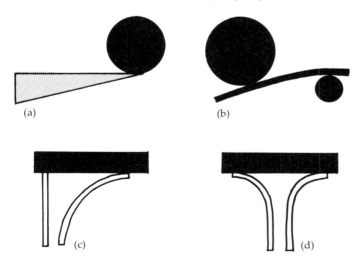

(a)   (b)

(c)   (d)

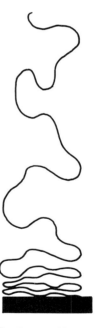

A moving line is stopped by a dense black bar. Since the line has become compressed against it some of the tension is resolved although it is still present.

Tension can be produced by conflicting visual weights or strengths.
   (a) The visual weight of the black disc is too heavy for the less dense triangle so tension is set up.
   (b) The visual weight appearing to bend the line causes tension.
   (c) One support is curved so that the heavy black bar seems to be collapsing to the right.
   (d) Here the tension is more resolved as both supports respond to the visual weight.

139

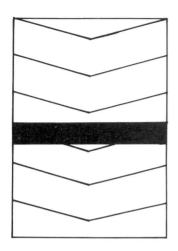

The strong dominant movement created by the chevron shape is held up by the dense black bar causing unresolved tension.

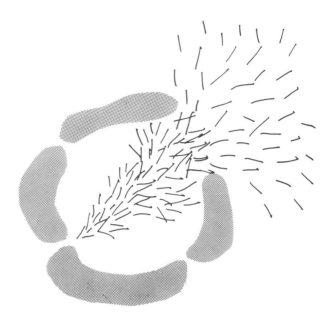

A bursting movement where the grey shapes have opened to let the small linear forms escape in an explosive way: resolved tension, although there is still a point at the mouth of the enclosing form where the movement is slowed up.

produce as much vitality as unresolved tension but is more harmonious. A line such as a road which responds to the visual forces running down a hill slope rather than cutting across it, the alignment of a shape with the direction of the forces acting upon it, a dominant form exerting influence on a weaker have resolved tension and yet maintain vitality.

Unresolved tension may be adapted for a particular purpose: for example, by an artist or sculptor who wishes to arouse particular emotions or sensations in the viewer. A moderate degree of tension might be used to unbalance the observer and enhance the dramatic effect of views or features suddenly appearing – raising expectations but fulfilling them in an unexpected way.

It is necessary to remember that forms which are in resolved physical tension (or compression) such as beams or girders in a bridge, may exhibit visual tension when seen from certain angles. Such confusion of elements can often be resolved by giving them a hierarchical pattern: for instance using colours to pick out particular parts such as the main structural components.

Rhythm

● If similar forms are repeated at intervals a rhythm will occur.

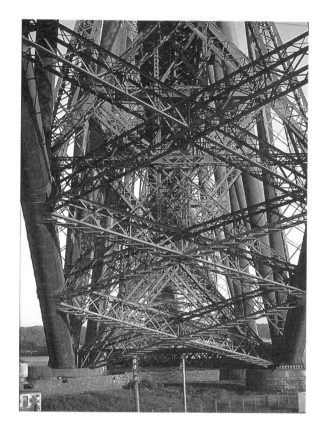

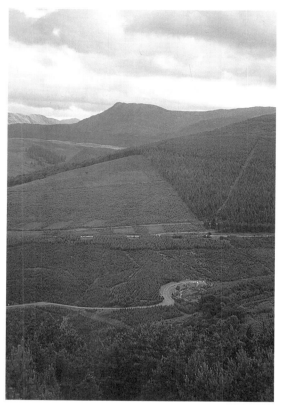

A view of the Forth Railway Bridge, Scotland, where the visual confusion caused by the view of the intersecting girders sets up tensions. This is caused partly by the lack of an obvious pattern or hierarchy of structure as well as the variable directions of the structural elements.

A plantation where the shapes conflict strongly with the underlying landform, particularly the triangular shape which shows a direction up towards the ridge while the main visual forces are running down the ridge (see Visual Force).

- Shape is a strong variable important in creating rhythms.
- Natural rhythms are more irregular than man-made ones.
- Rhythms can be simple or complex.
- Rhythm is used as an important structural device and brings a design to life.

Similar elements repeated at related regular or similar intervals create rhythms, especially when there is also a strong sense of direction involved.

Since shape is one of the strongest variables, repeating similar-shaped elements is one of the strongest means of producing rhythm. The type of shape can influence the way the rhythm develops: for example a line can have a lazy, slow movement or quick, staccato movement.

Structural elements

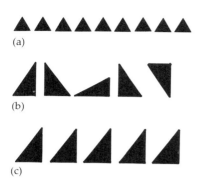

(a)

(b)

(c)

(a) A series of triangles repeated at the same interval: our eye runs along them picking up the interval and starts to read a rhythm.

(b) Another series of triangles which clearly do not have any rhythm owing to their varied positions and directions.

(c) The same triangles all repeated in interval and direction create a stronger rhythm than (a) because there is a clear movement from left to right.

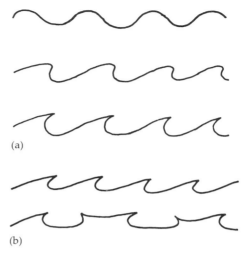

(a)

(b)

(a) Rhythm increases in each successive pattern as the directional emphasis increases.
(b) Two directions in the second pattern is also rhythmic but in staccato fashion.

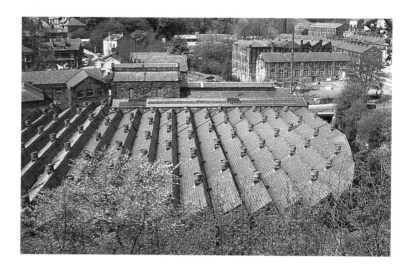

Factory roofs at Hebden Bridge, Yorkshire, England. There is a strong directional rhythm running from left to right across the roof owing to the shape and repetition. The ventilators also produce rhythms running in several directions. Together these create a very dynamic pattern.

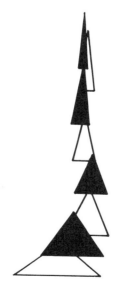

The changing shape of the triangle and the alternate black and white pattern sets up a rhythm with a direction from bottom to top.

Rhythms can occur in any direction. Linear horizontal rhythms are seen in roof shapes, lines of columns or trees shaped by the wind. Vertical rhythms occur in the repeated shapes of a church roof or tree crowns at different heights. They can also be three-dimensional as in the repetition of landform shapes. Man-made rhythms tend to be regular whereas in nature there is more irregularity: for example in ripple marks in the sand or seaweed

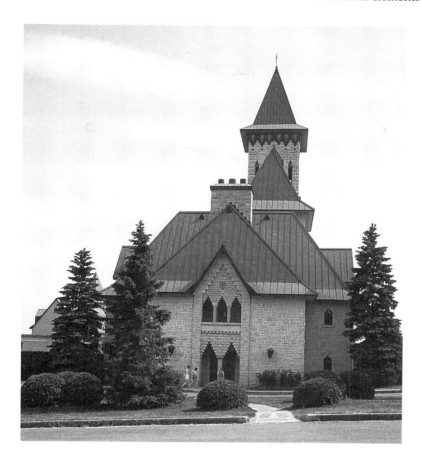

The repeated triangular shapes of the gables, windows, porch and roof shapes set up a rhythmical pattern from bottom to top, culminating in the spire. Smaller rhythms are set up in the triangular decoration of the stonework details. Monastery of St Benoit du Lac, Quebec, Canada.

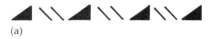

(a)

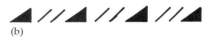

(b)

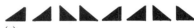

(c)

Rhythms may work in several directions at once, as long as one is stronger than another. The triangles in (a) are stronger than the lines, although the rhythms in (b) in one direction are easier on the eye. In (c) the equal strength of the two sets means that the rhythms are less easy to pick up.

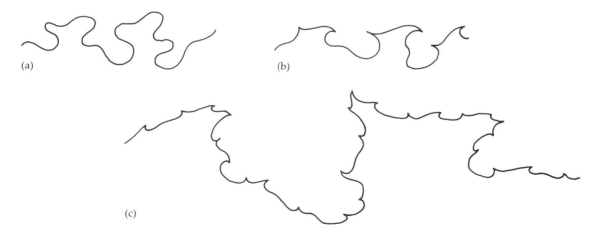

(a)

(b)

(c)

The pattern in (b) is a more dynamic rhythm because the eye can pick up the points and interpret them as a rhythm more easily. In (c) the idea is developed further with a major rhythm at a larger scale being repeated along the line at a smaller scale.

washed up on the shore reflecting the movement of the waves.

Rhythms can be composite, made up of clusters of repeated forms rather than just single ones. Repeated patterns of denser clusters of flowers in a field lead the eye from one to another; the result is a sort of swarming movement.

More complex rhythms involve one or more simple rhythms superimposed, such as when a generally sweeping, slower line is composed of a lot of smaller, faster moving shapes. This superimposition may also involve directional changes creating restless contrapuntal movement at the same or a different speed. This effect can create a very dynamic design but unless there is a hierarchy between the competing rhythms tension and disruption may result.

Rhythm can be a very useful device to help structure the parts of a composition. It is one of the chief means of bringing a design to life and can add a layer of refinement to an otherwise dull result. It is especially useful as a means of further enhancing a design relying on visual forces: for example a road, forest margin or any edge between two shapes which already to some extent reflect rhythms in the underlying landform. Many of the details in built design can be more successfully brought into the composition and given a decorative as well as functional part to play using rhythm. All of these aspects contribute strongly to unity by linking all the elements together.

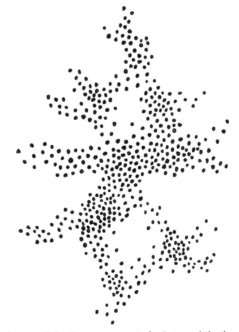

The edges of the shape made by the arrangement of points, and the denser clusters set up 'organic' rhythms.

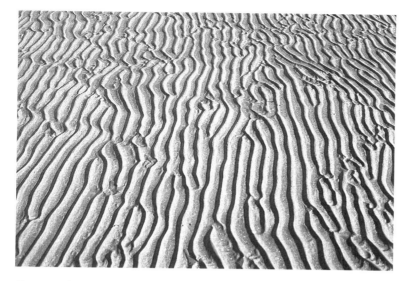

Ripples in the sand at a sea shore exposed following the receding tide have irregular rhythms which reflect the movement of the waves. The patterns vary over different parts of the beach.

Proportion

- Proportion concerns the relative size of elements or parts of elements to each other.
- Intuitive proportion relies on trial and error.
- Classical rules include the Golden Section, based on a rectangle of certain dimensions.
- A spiral results from extending the Golden Section and is found in many living organisms.
- The Pentagon and the Golden Triangle are related to the Golden Section.
- The Fibonacci Series of numbers also produces a logarithmic spiral.
- In art, architecture and formal landscape design the Golden Section is often used.
- In less formal landscapes the precise application of the Golden Section is impossible and the 'rule of thirds' can be substituted.

Any design or composition is made up of a number of elements or parts of elements. The relative sizes of these, that is the proportion in which they occur, is very important for achieving visual harmony and unity. Good proportion can be produced in a number of ways.

Although many methods for achieving good proportion rely on rules it is also possible to use a more intuitive approach based on trial and error. For example, the relative sizes of rectangles into which a square is subdivided can be found this way and produce a very harmonious result. Many designs rely on this method because the circumstances do not allow the application of the more formal approaches discussed below.

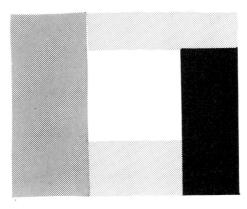

An example of 'intuitive' proportion – the relative sizes of the subdivisions of the shape are worked out so that they 'feel' right, so that they look comfortable. If such a composition were analysed it might approximate to some mathematical proportion.

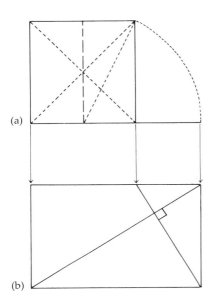

(a)

(b)

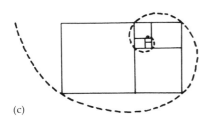

(c)

The Golden Section.
   (a) A square is extended using an arc from a point half way along one side.
   (b) The proportions of the rectangle thus formed, where the end of a line at right angles to the diagonal inside intersects the edge at the corner of the original square, corresponds to 1:1.618 where 1 = the length of the short side and 1.618 the length of the longer.
   (c) Adding a square to the longer side of the rectangle produces another rectangle conforming to the Golden Section. A line connecting the outer corners of each rectangle produces a logarithmic (constantly expanding) spiral, often known as the 'Curve of Life'.

From ancient times rules of proportion have been used based on various numerical ratios. The most important of these is the Golden Section which has been applied since the times of the ancient Egyptians and Greeks. The ratio 1:1.618 is used to create a rectangle whose shorter side is one unit and longer side 1.618 units long. Each time a square is subtracted from the original rectangle a smaller rectangle remains which has the same proportions. Conversely, a square can be added to the longer side to produce a larger-sized rectangle of the same proportion.

If the addition is continued an ever-increasing spiral formation results. This spiral is often called the 'curve of life' because it can be found in the growth pattern of many organisms such as mollusc shells and the arrangement and sizes of leaves around a plant stem. The spiral is logarithmic and grows at a constantly increasing rate determined by the Golden Section.

Other related features are the Pentagon whose proportions and angles are related to the Golden Section, and the Golden Triangle whose shape derives from the Pentagon and the Golden Section. The Golden Triangle was used by draughtsmen; it was a tool of more subtle proportions than the 30/60 degrees triangle commonly used today which is derived from the hexagon. The pentagon is also found as the basic shape in many plant forms such as the petal arrangements in many flowers.

A further mathematical series related to the Golden Section is the Fibonacci Series (1, 1, 2, 3, 5, 8, 13 etc.), in which each number is the sum of the two preceeding numbers (a phenomenon also of the Golden Section) (see Number). This also produces a logarithmic spiral seen in plant growth.

Attempts have been made to relate the proportions of the human figure to the Golden Section, for example by Leonardo da

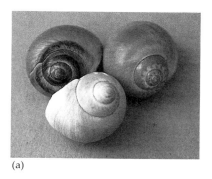
(a)

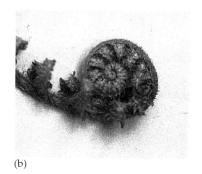
(b)

Two examples from nature of the 'Curve of Life':
  (a) the spiral line of growth of shellfish;
  (b) the frond of a fern gradually uncurls and expands: the shape thus formed is a
logarithmic spiral, and also corresponds to the Fibonacci series.

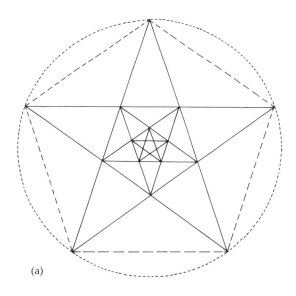
(a)

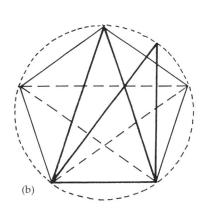
(b)

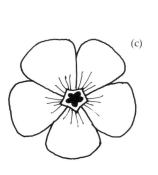

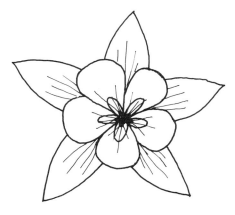
(c)

The pentagon: (a) the angles and proportions can be seen to correspond to the Golden Section. (b) The right-angled triangle which can be derived from the pentagon (the Golden Triangle) was used for drafting purposes in times gone by. (c) Two flower heads of five petals: the proportions of these conform to the pentagon and thus to the Golden Section.

147

Structural elements

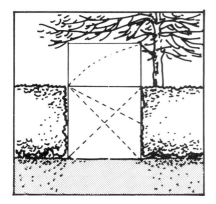

The Golden Section can be used in design to define the proportion of parts of a composition. Here the proportion of an opening and the height of the canopy of a tree are calculated according to it.

Vinci and more recently by Le Corbusier who produced a proportioning system based on a 1.829 m (6 ft) tall person, the Modulor.

The Golden Section has been used in architecture, in art, for composing the proportions and position of elements in a painting, and in landscape design, especially where a single viewpoint is involved. However, in many circumstances it is difficult to assess and use the Golden Section. Balance in many landscapes depends on how things look from many angles. The precise proportions of a plan or elevation such as of a garden layout or building façade are relatively easy to cope with.

Where views are variable in position and angle and where the landscape is more irregular, especially regarding landform, then a more pragmatic approach is desirable. This is the 'rule of thirds'. A derivation of the Golden Section, the rule is a simple guide to the general balance of proportions of elements in a composition: for example, open space to woodland or roof to wall. It seems to

The Parthenon in Athens: the proportion of the entire building and its subdivisions conform to the Golden Section.

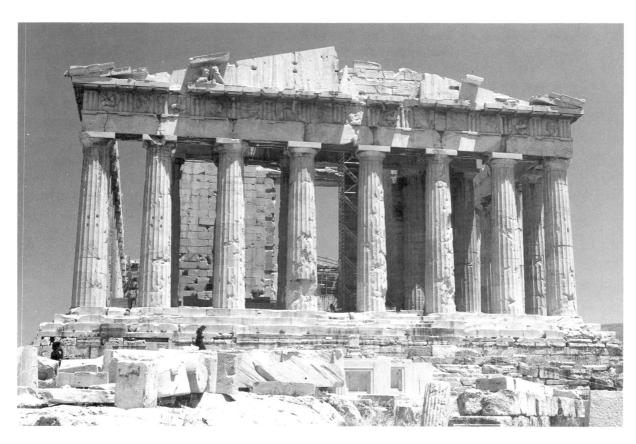

be generally more satisfactory for one part of a scene to dominate and unify the rest by occupying over 50% of the view. A 50:50 split between portions of a design does not allow one element to dominate and as a result tends to look uncomfortable, while more than two-thirds proportion tends to over-dominate and even become oppressive. Therefore a proportion of one third to two thirds generally seems to look better.

The rule is particularly useful in regulating the proportions of area or volume of elements as opposed to sizes and dimensions. A building façade may be split into thirds of, for example, roof plane to walls, doors to walls and one material to another. Areas of woodland in the landscape or areas of open space within a woodland may be organized so that they seem to occupy one third or two thirds of the view as seen from a number of points. This is not necessarily one third to two thirds as measured areas taken from a plan.

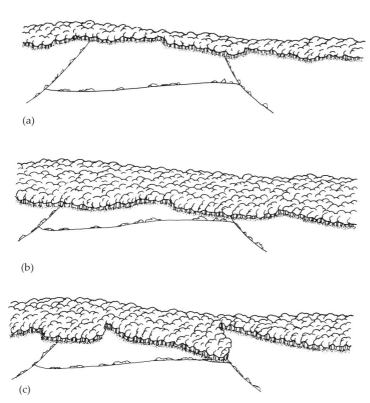

(a)

(b)

(c)

The rule of thirds.
(a) Less than one third woodland in this scene looks uneasy.
(b) A 50:50 split also looks uncomfortable: neither element is dominant.
(c) One third woodland to two thirds open ground below looks a better proportion.

149

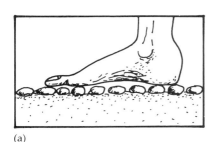

(a)

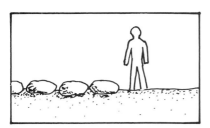

(b)

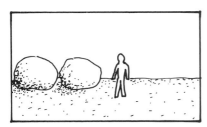

(c)

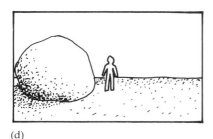

(d)

Scale is relative to the size of the human body.
  (a) The stones are seen as a ground surface: texture shows up.
  (b) They are seen as a cluster of rocks.
  (c) The boulders are the same size as the person – seen as individuals.
  (d) The rock is larger than the person, therefore it is difficult to assess the complete form.

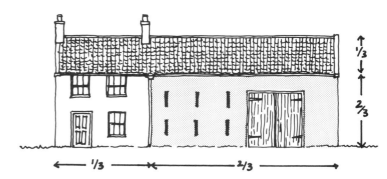

It is possible to subdivide the proportions of a building using the rule of thirds: here an old farmhouse and barn were built to approximate this rule in the roof/wall ratio and also the house/barn wall ratios.

The rule of three also has a history of use. The English landscape gardener Humphry Repton applied it when dividing masses of trees and open space into the correct proportions, and when designing planting layouts. Two thirds of an area would be planted with one species of tree and the remaining third by a mixture, in order to maintain the dominant element described above (see Diversity). It is an added benefit to the perception of harmony if the proportions of a composition can be seen both at a distance and close to (see Hierarchy).

Scale

- Scale concerns the sizes of elements relative to the human size and to the landscape.
- The size of an element cannot be assessed unless compared to ourselves or to an object of known dimensions.
- Scale is constantly adjusted as different parts of the landscape are viewed.
- Scale varies depending on size of landscape and the distance from the observer to it.
- Scale interacts with the degree of enclosure in the landscape.
- Designs need to be resolved at all scales because the background seen from one viewpoint becomes foreground seen from another.

Scale is related to proportion in that it involves visually balancing sizes and numbers of elements: between the elements of a design and the composition as a whole, with human size or with the landscape.

The most important aspect of scale is the way we perceive our surroundings in relation to our own size. We can only truly assess how big something is when we compare it to ourselves. We constantly adjust our perceptions of scale to take in the far distance, the middle ground and our immediate foreground simultaneously and the distances in between as a continuous gradation. This alters our perception of what we see and the degree of definition at which we see it. If there are no sudden breaks in the continuity of the scale hierarchy this looks more harmonious than if there is a sudden change from one scale to another.

Scale varies according to the distance of the observer from the landscape and the amount of landscape that can be seen, both in the horizontal and the vertical dimensions. A landscape can appear large-scale if much of it can be seen over long distances. The actual size of the landscape, for instance the height of a mountain, is not always a determining factor. A close landscape can also seem large-scale even though the vertical dimension is not very great if it occupies a large amount of the observer's field of view.

Since the scale of a space is a combination of height over distance, our feeling of enclosure depends on the height of the enclosing element and its distance from us. There are limits where an element of a given height is either too far away to provide enclosure or so close as to begin to feel oppressive.

Our perception of scale constantly shifts as we move from the distant view of mass/open space and sky where features appear

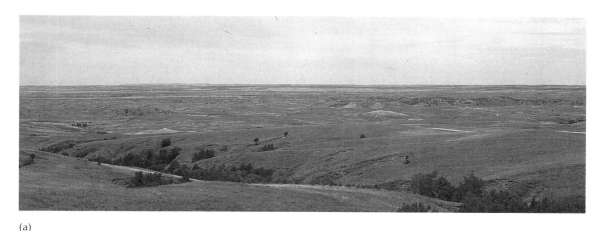

(a)

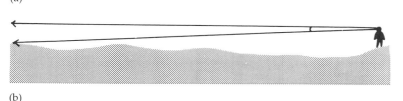

(b)

(a) An example of a large-scale landscape: the view takes in a great horizontal distance but the vertical variation is small. The Badlands National Park, South Dakota, USA.
(b) In this type of landscape the observer takes in the distance.

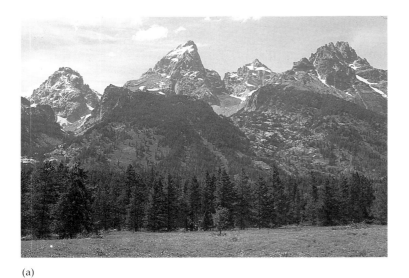

(a)

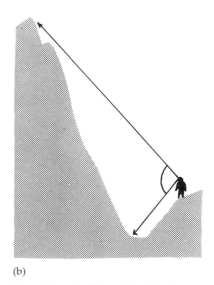

(b)

(a) A large-scale vertical landscape: height variation is large but distance is relatively small. Grand Tetons National Park, Wyoming, USA.
(b) The observer has to accommodate a wide cone of vision.

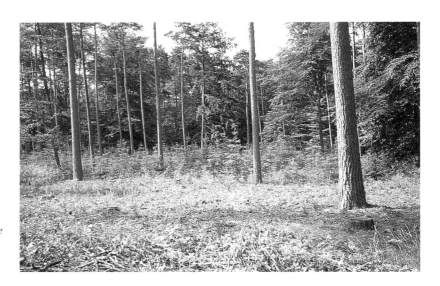

A small-scale landscape where the enclosure of the space by the trees is one of the important aspects to register. Breda, Holland.

as part of a pattern or texture (background) to middle distances where individual features stand out from the background and start to have texture and form in their own right (middle ground) to close distances where we concentrate on smaller objects and the details of the landscape (foreground). It follows that any design ranging across these scales needs to be resolved from all three distances since viewpoints shift and what is foreground in one view may become part of the background in another.

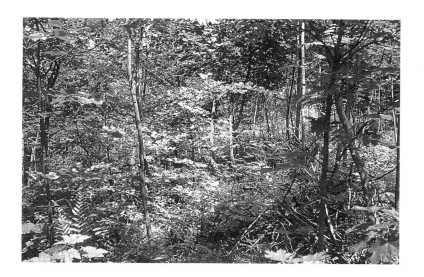

An intimately scaled landscape where the observer focuses on the details of the foreground: leaves, bark etc. The sense of space is lost.

The degree of scale of a space depends on its extent relative to the height of the enclosing or defining elements.
   (a) A wider space will seem larger in scale than . . .
   (b) . . . a narrower space where the enclosing elements are the same height. The degree of enclosure may seem oppressive or non-existent at the extremes.
   (c) and (d) The height of the enclosing elements relative to the space varies.

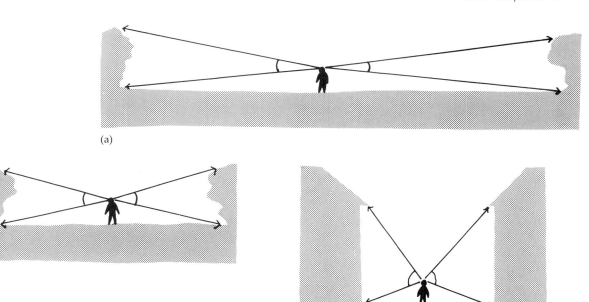

(a)

(b)

(c)

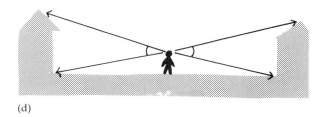

(d)

153

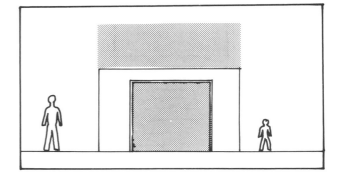

In isolation it is difficult to read the scale of an object: is this a big or a small building? We can only tell when there is a person or an object of known size near it.

The height of an observer also alters the perception of scale. An example could be views into and over a valley. Down in the valley bottom the distances are short, views limited and enclosure by landform strong, giving a sense of the small scale; viewed from high up on the summits of the hills surrounding it, the valley is seen as part of a landscape of much wider scale. Mid-way up the valley side the scale is somewhere in between, implying that there is a gradation of scale from valley bottom to hill top. This has important implications for design since small elements will tend to look out of scale if they are located at the

A house built to resemble an eighteenth century European mansion. In fact, although the proportions are correct, it is very small in scale compared with its models. This can be seen in the way the mature trees dwarf it. Mount Vernon, Virginia, USA.

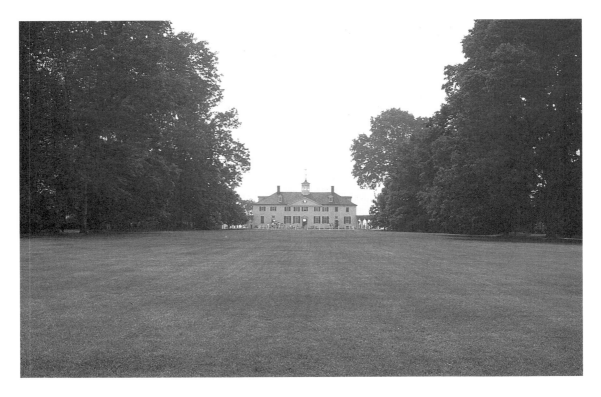

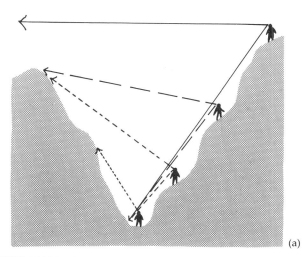

(a)

(b)

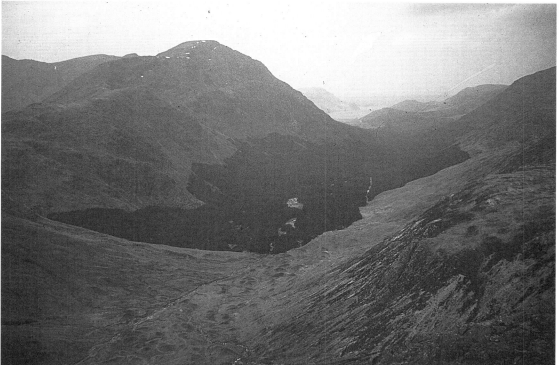

(a) The perception of scale in the landscape is determined by the position of the observer. The scale is perceived as small down in a valley bottom and gradually increases as more of the landscape can be seen and the sense of enclosure reduces, culminating in the view from the hill top where views extend well beyond the immediate valley.

(b) A view over a deep valley containing a forest as seen from the mountain tops. The scale is large seen from this point, but a person down in the valley bottom will perceive it as a much smaller scale. Design to accommodate the changes in scale can use small elements in the valley bottom which become progressively larger up the slopes towards the top of the hill.

155

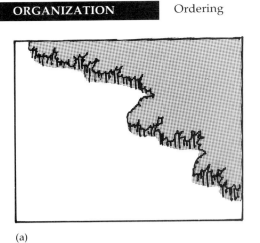

(a)

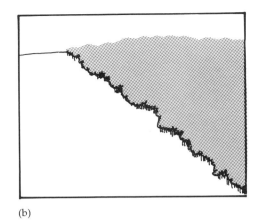

(b)

Scale and distance have their effects: in (a) the variation in shape along a woodland edge looks quite interesting yet from a viewpoint further away at (b) the overall impression is of a straight line with a few small-scale variations along it.

higher, bigger parts of the landscape where large elements will be in scale. Care is therefore needed to ensure that the scale of the landscape is taken into account during design. This is not easy to do unless the scale of all the viewpoints in any landscape where landform is important is assessed. In other cases scale can be tested by using simple rules of thumb of distance from the observer versus height of object and by using interlock and closure to control it.

Very large objects are difficult to fit into any but the largest-scale landscapes. For example, large power stations tend to dwarf everything around them. However, we need human-sized objects to be near them in order to register scale. If the design is kept simple and all the lower-level detail which would enable us to assess scale readily is screened from view it is possible to reduce the apparent scale and so lessen the impact.

Ordering

The next five principles are concerned with order in a design, landscape or composition. Any design requires some order in it but the application of the principles of Axis and Symmetry can result in very formal results. Hierarchy need not be so formal and is a useful device in any design. Datum is another way of organizing elements so that we pick up a pattern and Transformation is a method of introducing order across the boundaries between different patterns.

Axis

- An axis is a line about which elements are arranged.
- It is a very formalizing device in design.
- Axes are often found in design where symbolisms of power are displayed.

- An axis may be used to guide the eye from one part of a design to another.

An axis is a line, either real or implied and almost invariably straight, about which elements are arranged. It is a simple yet powerful device to create spatial order and discipline and one of the earliest to be used by ancient civilizations. At its most basic it may be the imaginary line connecting two focal points. The axis is more effective when reinforced or given spatial definition by enclosing elements alongside it. These may be built forms as in an urban setting, such as the Champs Elysées in Paris, or it may be in the form of an avenue of trees as in some of the great hunting forests of Europe.

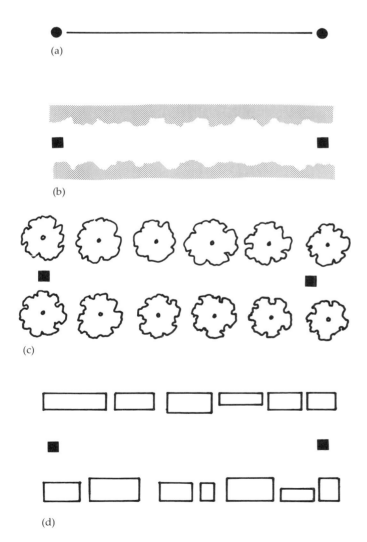

(a)

(b)

(c)

(d)

(a) The line, real or implied, between two points is an axis.
(b) An axis defined by a linear space between vegetation masses.
(c) An avenue of trees used to mark an axis.
(d) Built forms defining the space for an axis.

157

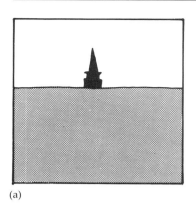

(a)

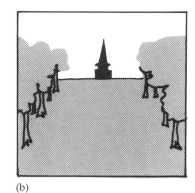

(b)

(a) A point feature on the horizon, the landform being flat.
(b) Parallel masses of trees define the space and create an axis which ties the point into the landscape.
(c) and (d) The same effect using less symmetrically arranged masses where the point is located on a hill.

The Grande Axe, an axis extending from La Defense through the Arc de Triomphe and down the Champs Elysées is a major feature of the urban layout of the city of Paris. Axes or boulevards were laid out as part of a grand design in the 1860s and impart a strong structure on the city.

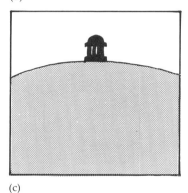

(c)

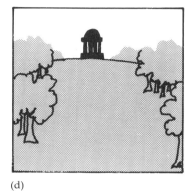

(d)

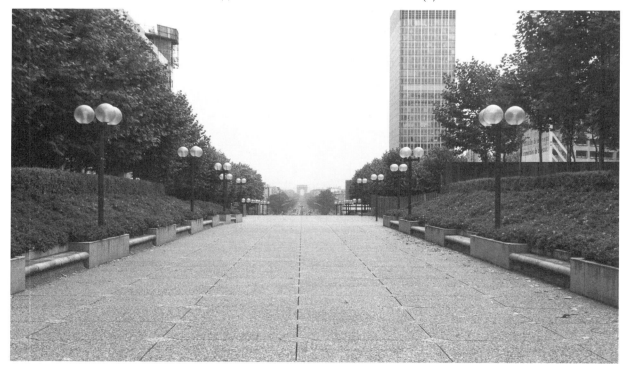

The axis is a very formalizing device in a design and can be used to impart very strong control over otherwise diverse elements. This is because it tends to dominate over other organizational aspects of a composition. As such it has been most used as a device where there is some sort of symbolic aspect to the design as in a classical landscape where man's dominance over nature is an important theme, such as at Versailles or where religious ceremonies and religious power are displayed such as at St Peter's in the Vatican City or in Pharaonic Egypt. Also implicit in some schemes is the symbolism of the autocratic state such as the massive redesign of Bucharest in Romania under the Communist regime into a huge axial arrangement, or the boulevards of Paris by Hausmann.

The use of axes may be mingled with other devices or tempered with a contrast of less rigid appearance. Sometimes the axis can be used to guide the eye from one part of a design to another. At Powerscourt in Ireland the axis begins at a very formal section of the gardens near the house and takes the eye over the terraces, with their great steps, across the lake and fountain to the landscape beyond and the Sugarloaf mountain in the distance. (See Case Study Two.)

The axis forming the ceremonial approach to St Peter's in Rome. The use of this device emphasizes the symbolic and real power of the Pope.

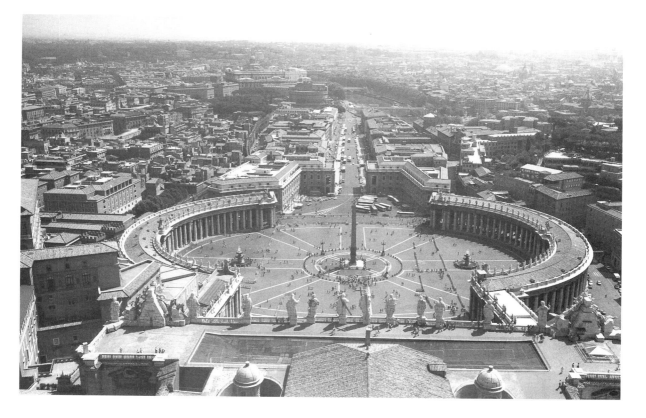

Avenues are a favourite device and are easy to create but they are not true axes unless they have a focal point towards which the eye is led.

Symmetry

- Symmetrical compositions tend to be very formal, stable and restful.
- Symmetry can be bilateral, kaleidoscopic or dualistic.
- Bilateral or 'mirror image' symmetry is the simplest and most commonly used form.
- Dualistic symmetry is less stable and tends to be used in fine art.
- Asymmetric designs, that is, ones lacking in symmetry are informal and can be less restful and unstable.
- Natural landscapes tend to be asymmetric.
- Symmetrical shapes in asymmetric landscapes can cause visual tension.
- Designs can combine symmetry and asymmetry if done in an ordered way.

Symmetry is another principle concerned with the relationship of parts of a composition to the whole and the balance between them. Symmetrical compositions tend to appear very formal, stable and restful while asymmetrical designs represent the opposite – unstable, although not necessarily unbalanced, restless and informal.

Bilateral symmetry, where each half of an object is the mirror image of each other across a median line, is the most commonly found type. It is also the simplest. It is found in the human body, in many leaves, in some flowers and is used in conjunction with an axis in many garden designs. In classical architecture it is an important component. In the natural landscape it is rarely found. Some glaciated valleys are almost perfectly U-shaped in cross-section, but usually there is a high degree of asymmetry in landform since erosive forces tend to work in a particular direction.

Kaleidoscopic symmetry also involves the repetition of exactly corresponding parts but of more than two arranged around a central node. In nature this is found more commonly – in many flowers, and in simple animals such as jelly fish. In built forms it is used extensively, as in domed buildings. In gardens it is to be found in complex parterres, particularly in classical designs.

The third kind of symmetry is referred to as dualistic, where an image or form consists of two halves which are not quite identical and tend to compete with each other. The eye tries to fuse them into a single form so it is not as stable as the other types. It has

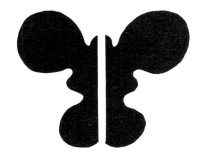

An example of bilateral symmetry where the shape is repeated across the median line in one plane only.

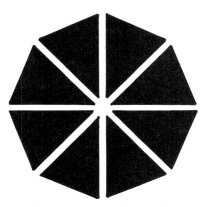

Kaleidoscopic symmetry: there are three lines across which each part is reflected.

been used in fine art where a particular ambiguity is desired. It can also be symbolic of the duality which exists in many things such as the ying and the yang, the positive and the negative.

Asymmetry tends to be found in natural landforms, in plant growth as a result of external forces, in natural vegetation caused by fire and wind in natural forests. When man-made shapes in natural landscapes are symmetrical this is one more reason why

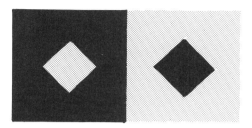

Dualistic symmetry: our eyes try to transpose the black diamond back into the black space and vice versa.

An example of bilateral symmetry at Hidcote Manor gardens in Gloucestershire, England. The line of symmetry extends from the viewer up the steps and is carried on by the pleached hornbeam hedges. The symmetry extends to the plants on either side of the steps, the two buildings and even down to the small wire fences to prevent members of the public from straying!

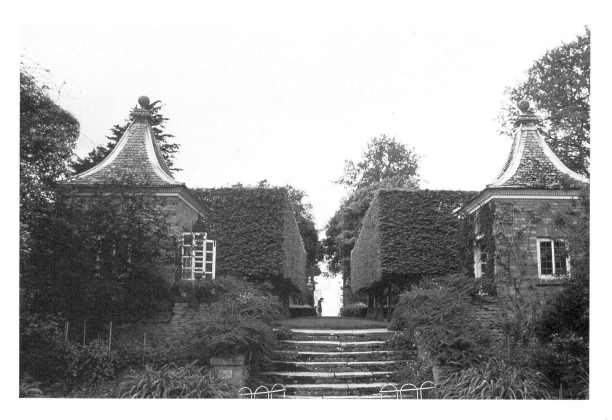

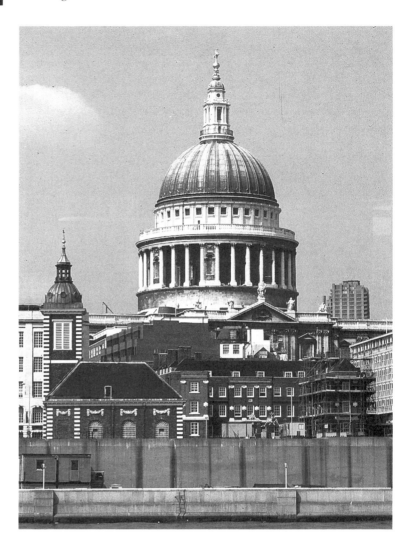

St Paul's Cathedral, London. The dome is composed of segments around a central point. This is a prime example of kaleidoscopic symmetry.

visual tension and loss of unity can result, especially when landforms are strongly asymmetrical. The compatibility of the shapes is reduced or eliminated (see Shape).

In many designs asymmetry is used to create less formal, more relaxed results. Occasionally a mixture of the two is used. A building may consist of one section which is completely symmetrical and another section which makes the whole asymmetrical. Asymmetry may also be the result of a building responding to its site rather than imposing on it, for example stepping down the slope of a hill. Buildings which have grown over time in an irregular fashion will also tend to be asymmetric.

Hierarchy

- Many aspects of design require some parts to be visually dominant.
- Many natural patterns show visual hierarchy related to function or ecology.
- There is a hierarchy related to landscape scale.
- In settlement patterns the visual hierarchy can be derived from a social structure, from planning zoning or due to economic factors.
- Communication patterns are hierarchical.
- Architecture uses hierarchy of space and function.
- Decoration can be given a hierarchy.

As we have seen, many aspects of design require that some parts are clearly more important or visually dominant over others. This implies that in more complex compositions a clear hierarchy is

An example of an originally symmetrically designed house which has had an extension added on to one side. This has created an asymmetrical composition which remains balanced, since the general form is continued but stepped back to allow the original house to read. Belle Grove Plantation, Virginia, designed by Thomas Jefferson.

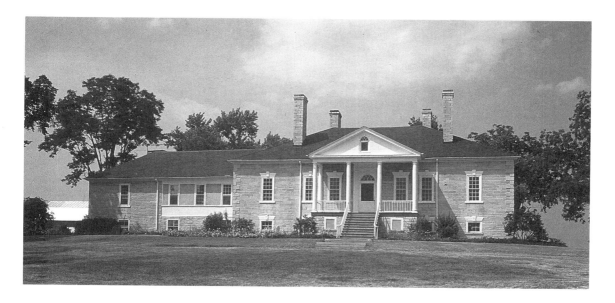

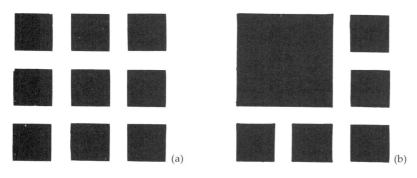

(a)

(b)

(a) A grouping of square planes where none of them is any more important than the others.
(b) One square is much larger and imposes a hierarchy on the rest, so a sense of order becomes established in the composition.

desirable to establish order in the relationship of the parts to the whole. This may be achieved by the application of many of the organizational principles dealt with so far. It is also useful to show how the minor details of a design relate to its major structural sections.

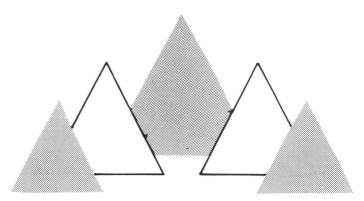

The positions and increasing sizes of the triangles imposes a hierarchical order on this grouping.

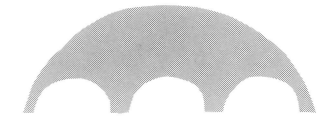

A single form provides an overall structure for the repeated shapes beneath.

Hierarchy is often found in nature and this helps us to understand the functional and ecological patterns there. A stream pattern may show a clear ordering of importance from the small streams emerging from springs through increasingly larger ones resulting from the confluence of the smaller until a large river results. In a vegetation pattern certain species or assemblages are dominant in some areas: for example, trees in a forest.

There are hierarchies of scale from hill top to valley bottom. This can be used to guide design of, for example, woodland where bigger areas are located on the hilltops, with smaller ones tucked in beneath (see Scale). A hierarchy has also been seen historically in field patterns where larger fields are necessary on the higher, less fertile lands than down in the richer valleys, although with modern farming machinery it has begun to work the other way, the biggest fields being on the best soils.

In settlement patterns there is often a clear hierarchy in the position and size of certain buildings such as the church or temple, the castle or mansion in relation to the farms and villagers' houses. This is not only a visual but also a social hierarchy, symbolic of power and influence. Hierarchies also develop due to planning and economic factors: for example, where a city centre has the financial, office-based sector, industry is located further out from this zone, and beyond it are the residential areas.

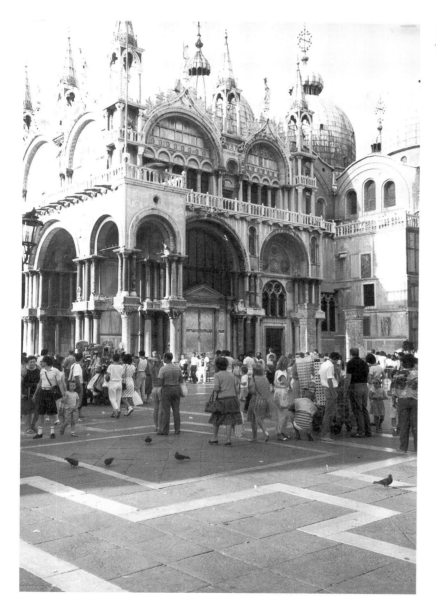

St Mark's, Venice: the use of repeated forms (arches) is given order by their hierarchical arrangement.

Ordering

A functional hierarchy can be found in roads, paths and other communication networks related to their importance. This creates a visual pattern as does the structure of the landscape in response to these, especially in places like the USA where the land-use pattern has been recently laid out with everything related to the grid. The location of freeways, highways and other roads of lesser importance is derived from or obviously cuts across the grid.

In architecture, a hierarchy is used in terms of spaces, forms and functions. A large form may be split into several smaller ones

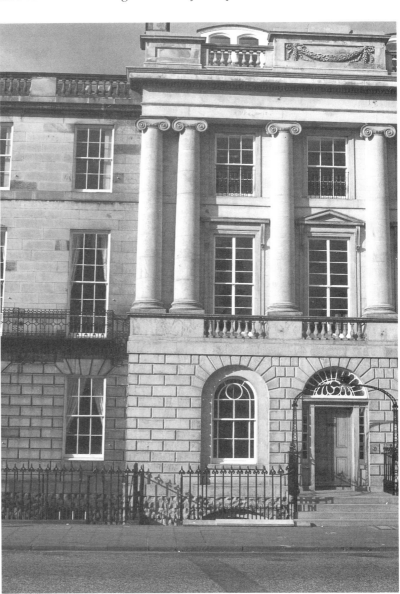

The design of this house façade shows a hierarchy of finishes and and textures, from the 'rusticated' stonework pattern on the basement, to progressively finer textures and the high orders of classical columns used as decoration. The result breaks down the scale and proportion of the façade and introduces a degree of detail which can be read from different distances and at a range of scales. New Town, Edinburgh.

where there is a dominant and several decreasingly sub-dominant parts. Decoration may also show a hierarchy, for instance in the horizontal layering of a Georgian house where the type of stone finish and the classical orders on the pilasters vary from 'rustic' on the lowest level to highly finished Corinthian on the upper storeys. Colours can also be given order in chroma and value which is hierarchical and related to function: for example, doors painted a bright colour, walls the next brightest and roofs darkest.

Datum

- A datum is a basic element used as a reference for other component elements in design.
- A point can act as a centre around which elements are arranged or from where they are controlled.
- A line is commonly used as a datum in a variety of ways, both real and implied.
- A plane provides a reference for the position of other elements.
- Solid and open volumes act in similar fashion to points and planes.
- Time can act as a datum for events and change in the landscape.

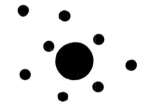

A large point (or small plane) acting as a datum around which a number of smaller points are clustered.

Datum refers to the use of a point, line, plane or volume to which the spatial organization of a design or composition and in particular the component elements can refer.

A point can act as a centre around which elements revolve such as the Sun controlling and organizing the planets of the Solar System or an axle point around which the moving parts of a machine rotate. It can also provide a central node around which elements cluster. An example of this might be a church tower acting as the focal point of a village. A volume may also act in this way. A point may also provide a datum from which elements radiate, such as a lighthouse providing a reference point for ships at sea. Paths radiating out from a nodal point are also provided with a datum. Another example of a datum point is the 'Meridian' at Salt Lake City in Utah, the point from which the whole city layout is organized and from which all the streets are numbered and named.

A line is more commonly used as a datum than any other element. It may be a real line such as a road or path along which houses or settlements are arranged, or the edge of a plane as in an urban square around which various buildings are located and organized. In Shape it was shown that the eye tries to pick out organization from apparent chaos and that identifying shapes is one powerful aspect of this.

Ordering

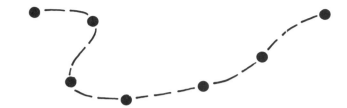

An implied line joining points into a structure.

The imaginary line passing from one element to another which we then see as a shape may also be considered as a datum. A circle may consist of stones placed at wide intervals but we are able to identify a line connecting them and identify them as a pattern conforming to a certain order.

The use of planes as datums can be seen in many examples. The floor plane is used to organize objects placed upon it, for example sculptures on a lawn, while a wall plane can provide a background against which to arrange elements such as windows and doors.

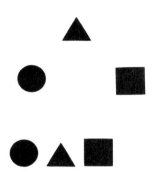

(a) Three small planes which are not structured in their position.
(b) Aligning them along a horizontal plane gives them structure.

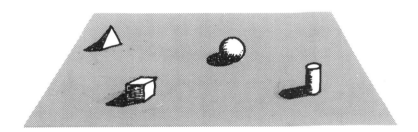

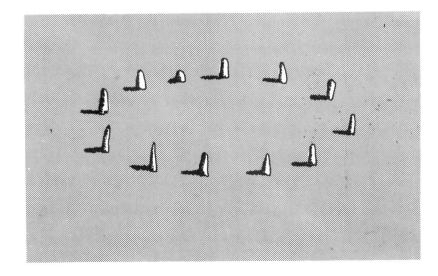

(a) A floor plane acting as a datum on which some small volumes are positioned.
(b) The ground plane used as a datum for the location of stones which themselves are arranged around an imaginary circle.

A wall plane acting as a datum for windows and a door.

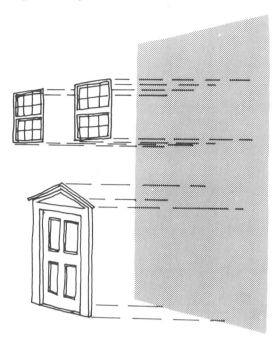

These statues in the gardens of the Palace of Versailles, France, occupy niches in the hedge so that it acts as a datum which partially encloses them. In addition the edge of the pool acts as another datum line since the row of statues is also seen in reflection. Furthermore the plane of the water surface acts as a datum for the fountain (not working when the photograph was taken) and in fact for the whole complex composition. The trees in the background can also be seen in relation to the hedge line.

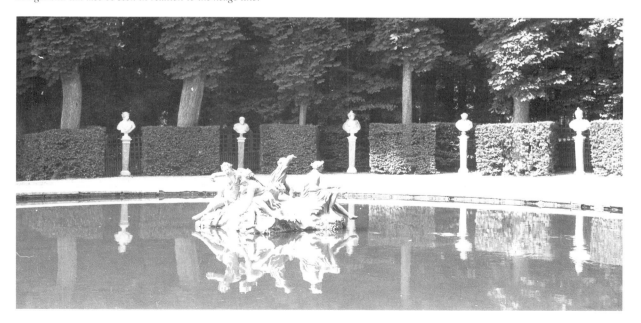

An imaginary datum plane is the survey datum used to mark zero height by cartographers – sea level, for example – and which is used to organize the land in relation to it.

Volumes provide a datum both as solids around which elements are arranged in a similar fashion to points, and as open volumes such as a wide, flowing roof which collects, organizes and encloses a number of elements. Such volumes must have sufficiently strong form, usually fairly simple, in order to read as the more dominant element (see Hierarchy). The canopy of a forest, the continuous roof of a large factory, airport terminal or stadium perform this function.

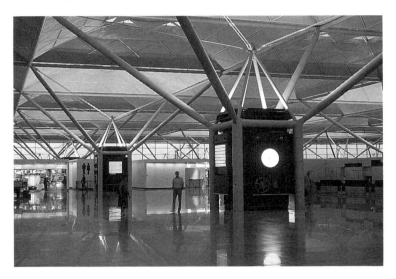

An open volume which encloses a space occupied by a disparate range of objects – desks, shop units, seating etc., which is all free-standing and self-contained. The volume thus acts as a datum to which these all relate, thus containing them. Stansted Airport, Essex, England.

Time is often perceived as linear in nature (from past to future via the present) providing a line of continuity along which events take place. In this way it can act as a datum (a base time or starting point) for growth, decay, process and change in the landscape.

Transformation

- Variation of function, scale or changes over time may show a logic in their spatial or temporal organization which can be identified as transformation.
- Natural patterns or land uses transform from one to another.
- Scenes transform over time.
- Transformation is used in design to reflect different characters, moods or parts of the landscape.

Many parts of the landscape or of a design differ in function, scale, natural process or because of development over time. If the

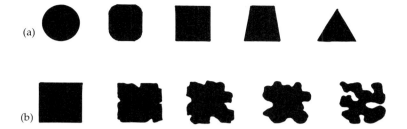

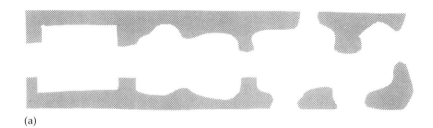

(a) Transformation of shape from a circle via a square to a triangle with transitional shapes in between.
(b) A geometric shape gradually transforms into an organic shape.

(a)

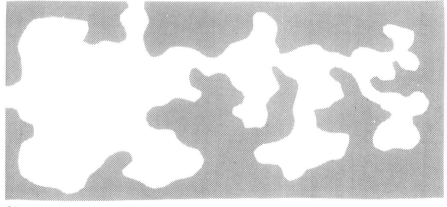

(b)

(a) The transformation of space from a geometric, formal shape into a more organic, less formal, less symmetrical shape. This type of transformation has been used in garden or park design for many years.
(b) Space/mass transformation: from predominantly space with little mass on the left to mostly mass with smaller amounts of space on the right.

various spatial or temporal variations are ordered into a logical sequence then quite often we can perceive transformation occurring.

In the natural world there are spatial transformations from one pattern to another such as from open water to dry land via degrees of wetland, or from prairie to forest by a gradual change in the amounts of woodland and numbers of trees. Land-use patterns show transformations in the gradual shift in intensity of cultivation or grazing as soil and climatic conditions change. These transformations are harmonious and ordered, closely reflecting the physical conditions.

Transformations with time can be seen in many circumstances. For example, the metamorphosis of a caterpillar into a butterfly, the growth of plants, changes in fashion or the use of materials. We see a recently ploughed field transform into a sea of bright green shoots, into waving golden heads of grain and into cut stubble all in a relatively short space of time.

Designers of gardens and parks have long used transformation in the emphasis of spatial design (formal to informal, small to large scale, geometric to irregular) exemplified by the transition

A landscape pattern which gradually transforms from well-tended, smooth green fields in the valley bottom up through irregular textured grass to scrubby woodland and rough woodland on the hill tops. Scale also transforms – small fields lower down, a larger-scale pattern higher up. Snowdonia National Park, Wales.

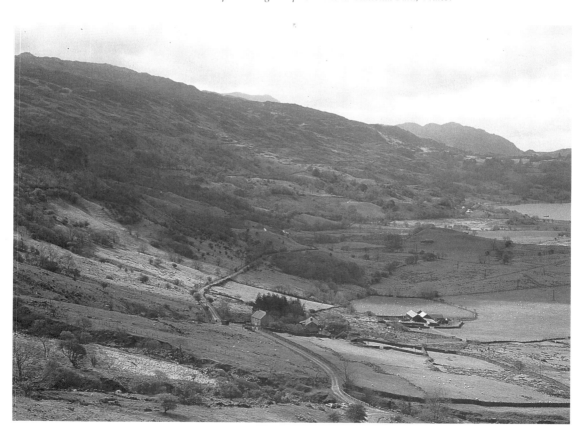

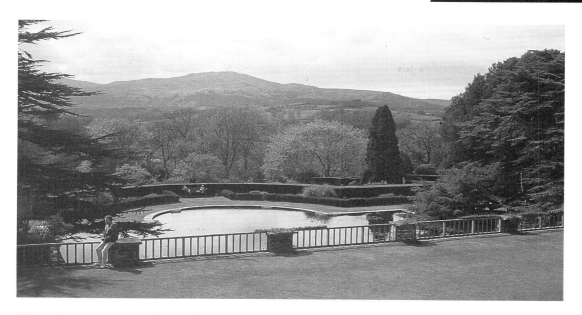

The transformation seen here is that of a formal garden seen in the foreground through parkland to a view of more distant mountain tops, symbolic of a wilder landscape. Bodnant Gardens, Gwynedd, Wales.

from the very formal layout of garden, ponds, statuary and clipped hedges close to the classical architecture of a fine house to less formal parkland further away. In designs reflecting the more natural landscapes transformation may be used in a different way. In a forest it may be desirable to use a variety of shapes ranging from regular ones near strong field patterns to more natural, irregular ones on the upper slopes where landform shapes and naturalistic vegetation patterns take over as dominant factors.

Transformations, evident both in time and space, are found in many towns and cities which have developed over a long period. Travelling from the Roman or medieval core of an old town in England to the modern, outer suburbs can involve passing through the street layouts and architectural styles of many intervening periods arranged in a more-or-less linear sequence.

4

Case Studies

Case Study 1:
Museum of Civilization, Ottawa, Canada

Case Study 2:
Powerscourt, Co Wicklow, Ireland

Case Study 3:
Strathyre Forest, Stirlingshire, Scotland

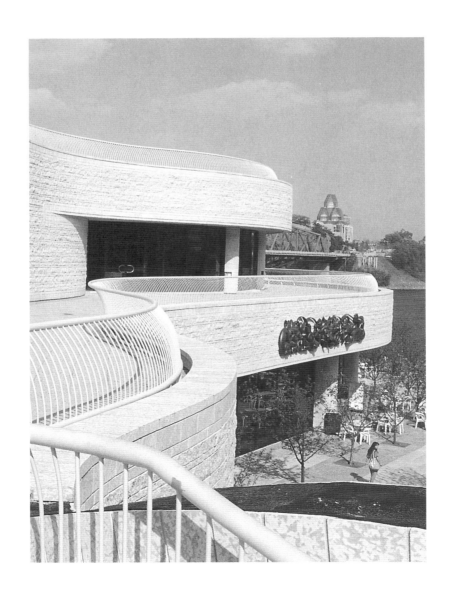

4

Case Studies

U_p to this point we have tended to look at examples in the light of particular design principles. Chapter 3 stressed the need for the three objectives of visual design to be met, namely unity, diversity and *genius loci*. Now it is appropriate to put together everything we have looked at so far and to look in some detail at three case studies.

The examples have been chosen to reflect completely different aspects of design: the first is primarily architectural, the second is a large-scale garden and the third concerns design in a rural, fairly wild landscape.

In each case study we can see how the design has been built up, what are the main influences at work and how the result fulfils the objectives of design.

Case study 1:
Museum of Civilization, Ottawa, Canada

The Canadian Museum of Civilization at Ottawa, the capital of Canada, was completed in 1989 to the design of the Canadian architect Douglas Cardinal. It emerged as a design in 1983 as the result of a competition although the end result has departed substantially from the earliest concept.

The site

The site layout has been determined in part by its location in Parc Laurier which is on the banks of the Ottawa River, on the Hull, Quebec side, opposite the Federal Houses of Parliament and other government buildings. The other major site-related influence is the straight line of the ceremonial route of Rue Laurier running parallel to the river and the axis running across the river to the Peace Tower.

The site had been identified as a museum site for some years. It

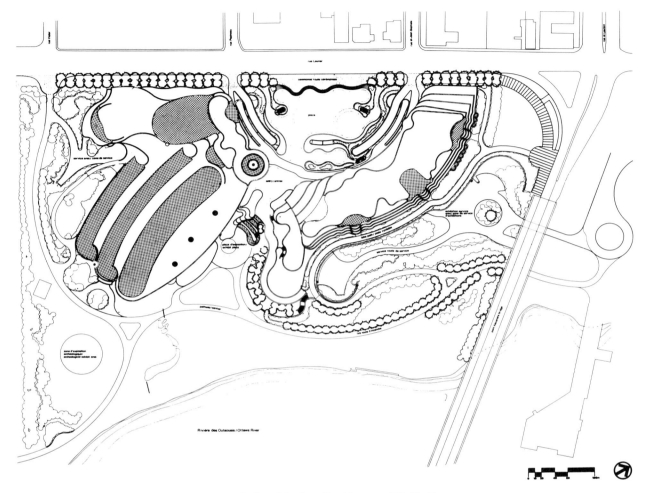

A plan of the Canadian Museum of Civilization.

is 9.6 ha in size although about half is prone to flooding. To the south is a forest products factory, to the north the Alexandria Interprovincial Bridge and Rue Laurier is to the west. The site therefore faces east across the river providing a panoramic view of the Parliament Buildings and the limestone escarpment upon which they sit.

The site is well served with access routes mainly from Rue Laurier and all car parking is underground – a response both to site limitations and climatic considerations. The result is that the design of the buildings is not compromised to any great extent by the site thus allowing an enormous degree of creativity to be unleashed.

The basic composition of the site consists of two buildings which enclose an open space or plaza over the car parking area.

This enables the buildings to be appreciated from the approach on Laurier Street. The buildings open out at angles to each other down the sloping river bank from where they form a composition capable of being appreciated from across the river, the open angle being on the Peace Tower axis.

Origins of the design

This work represents the first major building by Douglas Cardinal outside the plains provinces. To look at the origins of the design we must consider several factors. Firstly, the building is a museum. The role of museums in a country like Canada, which is a nation of immigrants from diverse backgrounds, is important for preserving and interpreting the past experiences of all the people. There is, therefore, a strong symbolism associated with the museum. Cardinal responded to this by designing a 'modern artefact', not merely a building to house exhibits. The second factor is the provenance of the architect. Douglas Cardinal is a 'landscape-inspired' architect. He considers the first step in architectural design to be to reach an understanding and feeling for the land on which a building will stand (Macdonald, 1989). As he has said:

> Instead of viewing the museum as a sculptural problem, instead of identifying all the historical forms and making them the vocabulary for my solutions, I prefer to take a walk in nature, observe how nature has solved its problems, and let it be an inspiration to me in solving mine.

> Our buildings must be part of nature, must flow out of the land: the landscape must weave in and out of them so that, even in the harshness of winter, we are not deprived of our closeness with nature.

This can clearly be seen in the outcome of the building. Cardinal is also clearly influenced more by the flowing art-nouveau forms of the Spanish architect Gaudi than the main movements of Post-Modernism prevalent at the time.

The third factor to be taken into account is the strategy for the interior of the museum. There is a heavy emphasis on simulation and pastiche for the set-piece recreations of Canadian life inside the exhibits. Rather than go for a design which quotes, in Post-Modern idiom, references to the function such as used by Michael Graves, or for a 'deconstructed museum' like Gehry, Cardinal used the opportunity to render symbolically the building as 'landscape mythically transformed', providing a base upon which to show the development of civilization in Canada – in

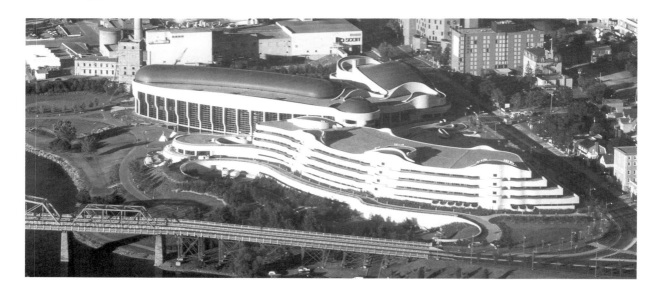

An aerial view of the two wings showing the distinctive organic shapes, the layered effect resembling rock strata of the Canadian Shield Wing and the more massive structure of the Glacier Wing behind. (Courtesy of Canadian Museum of Civilization.)

other words, the building represents the geology of Canada 15 000 years ago before man came, following the Ice Ages.

In terms of visual elements the composition is dominated by the two solid volumes of the buildings seated on the sloping plane of the ground surface. It is the form of the buildings which first strikes the visitor, made all the more emphatic by the simplicity of the surrounding landscape. It is immediately clear that the forms are derived from sources far removed from the usual references for architecture – in this case the two dominant factors in the make-up of the Canadian landscape, the Canadian Shield rocks and the effects of glaciation.

The Canadian Shield consists of ancient, mostly very hard rocks which have been eroded to form the relatively low relief of the majority of Canada with the main exception of the Rocky Mountains. This is reflected in the Canadian Shield Wing, the administrative and curatorial part of the museum, where the form is based on a series of layers, some forming terraces, reminiscent of rock strata. This can also be seen in the actual rocks of the limestone bluff along the river bank opposite, where the Parliament buildings rise. The plan shape is very organic, the walls curving in a rhythmic fashion, emphasized by the railings along the terraces and by the rough-textured stonework of the cladding. This form is similar to eroded rock strata which have been exposed to the force of glaciation yet whose horizontal direction remains strong and emphatic.

The Glacier Wing has an altogether different form, representing the dynamic force of moving ice as opposed to the static, stable rocks of the Shield. This is reflected in the plan shape comprising three linear, slightly curving segments and the building façade which is a massive vertical structure broken by columns at intervals along its length. This contrasts strongly with the horizontal, stepped façade of the Canadian Shield Wing. The overall form is best appreciated from within, from the Grand Hall which looks out and across the Waterfall Court to the Canadian Shield Wing. The hall thus becomes a vast open volume some three storeys high. The huge columns support a roof whose bold modelling reinforces the dynamic effect and the muscular strength of the whole emphasizes the derivation of the form from the glacier. The space itself could be a crevasse or tunnel within the ice. As well as this, there are evocations in some of the forms of native longhouses, earth lodges and igloos.

A close-up view of part of the terrace of the Canadian Shield Wing. The curving shapes create very interesting rhythms. The texture of the cladding is also evident.

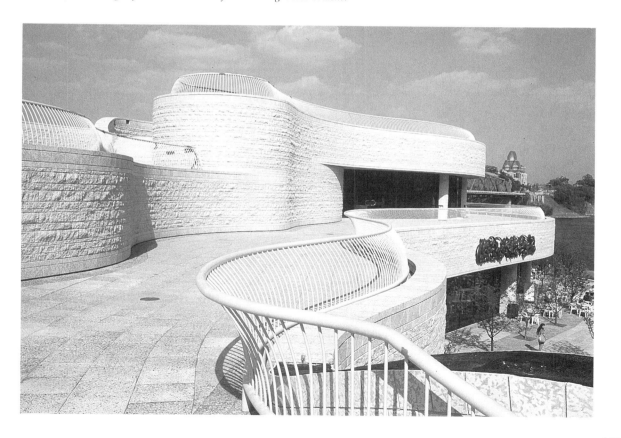

(a) The main entrance to the Glacier Wing, showing the distinctive form. (b) Elevation of the Glacier Wing showing the various forms and roof lines.

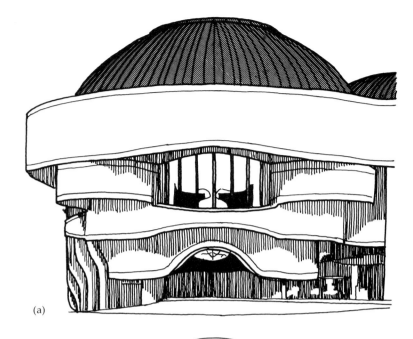

(a)

(b)

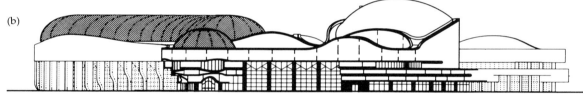

The modelling of the façade relies on the fenestration to emphasize the form, and to a much lesser extent on the detail of the cladding. The windows of the Canadian Shield Wing are horizontally arranged and recessed to create shadow and to emphasize the stratification of the layers of rock. The vertical direction of the windows of the Glacier Wing, also recessed to set off the columns, tends to give a definite rhythm and sense of movement and visual energy to the building. This is reinforced by the sculpting of the columns into sections of different thicknesses at different heights.

Colour has been kept deliberately simple and natural. There are slight differences due to the textural variations in the cladding stone, a limestone from Manitoba, which reflect light differently. This simplicity is appropriate, given the strength and scale of the overall concept and the main forms. Too much diversity in colour and texture would have tended to reduce scale and created fussiness where simplicity is necessary. It is as if the pure, clean ice of the Glacier has exposed the fresh rock to view for the first time. Weathering of the buildings will allow the action of time to proceed naturally, both on the rock of the Canadian Shield Wing and on the ice of the Glacier which, in real life, usually gets dirty as time goes by. The roof of the Glacier Wing is clad in copper which makes a visual connection with the roofs of the Parliament buildings across the river.

The building forms have been picked up in the organic shapes of the plaza off Laurier Street and in the Waterfall Court outside the Glacier Wing – reminiscent of the meltwater emerging from beneath a glacier. Elsewhere the design of the park between the building complex and the Ottawa River has been kept simple and uncluttered to allow the two forms to be seen together and to allow the eye to play over the two contrasting but nevertheless strongly unified elements.

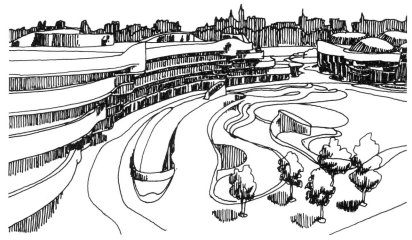

A view of the two wings looking across the river to the skyline of the Parliament buildings.

The composition has departed from its first inspiration as a result of the museum function, the cost and the fast-track construction schedule. It is impressive to see just how well the initial concept is respected and how the building really is a piece of sculpture, redolent of the land. It is also reminiscent of the organic forms used by Gaudi in the same way (the towers of the Sagrada Familia in Barcelona echo the rock pinnacles at Monserrat), although executed in a bolder, larger scale. In essence the result appeals to the 'national connection with the natural order addressed . . . to the ghost of the widerness that haunts (the Canadian) collective psyche' (Boddy, 1989).

References

Boddy, T. (1989) *The architecture of Douglas Cardinal*, NeWest Press, Edmonton, Alberta.
Macdonald, G.F. (1989) *A museum for the global village*, Canadian Museum of Civilization, Hull, Quebec.

Case study 2:
Powerscourt, Co Wicklow, Ireland

The formal gardens at Powerscourt House in the Wicklow Mountains of the east of Ireland, although established in a number of phases, nevertheless comprise a masterly overall composition which is both highly organized and structured yet also contains informality. While there are diverse gardens a strong sense of unity pervades the whole.

The gardens were begun shortly after the grand Palladian house was built, in 1743, by the first Viscount Powerscourt. The next phase commenced in 1843 under the sixth Viscount who

A site plan of Powerscourt.

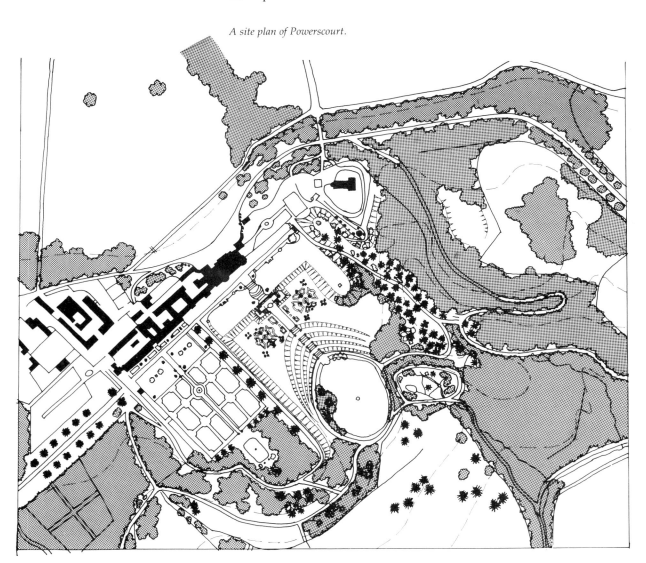

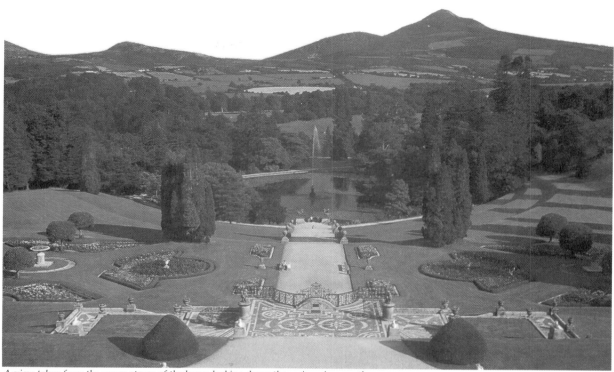

A view taken from the upper storey of the house looking down the main axis, over the Triton Fountain and out to the countryside beyond. The peak of the Sugarloaf Mountain is offset to the axis and provides a harmonious asymmetric balance to the formality of the foreground composition. (Courtesy of Powerscourt Trust.)

commissioned the architect Daniel Robertson to design and construct the terraces immediately to the south of the house. Fourteen years later in 1858, after the death of the sixth Viscount in 1844, the work was continued by the seventh Viscount with the creation of the formal parterres designed by Milner, an assistant of Joseph Paxton. In the late 1860s the lower terraces were constructed by Alexander Robertson and the Italianate Garden was completed in 1875 with the addition of the central Perron and fountains.

This most formal part of the garden is axially arranged from the centre of the garden front of the house towards the south-east. The eye is led down the path and steps which proceed in a grand manner from the upper terrace, down the Perron, past the parterres and on down the lower terraces to the Triton fountain in the middle of the lake. Trees help to hold the eye to the line. The axis is not continuous as a physical line beyond the Pegasi at the foot of the lower terraces but nevertheless retains a strong influence. The masses of trees flanking the lake continue the axis out of the gardens and park to the landscape beyond. Here the principal feature is the pinnacle of the Sugarloaf Mountain which is not directly on the axis – too obvious a device – but offset, adding an asymmetrical balance to what is otherwise a strongly symmetrical composition. This is appropriate since the strong formality created by man dominating nature in the gardens should contrast with the wilder, semi-natural landscape beyond, where the form of the mountain dominates.

Parts of the formal gardens, such as the Perron, are smaller self-contained compositions in their own right but are neverthe-less tied strongly into the rest of the design by the lines and planes of the terraces and the axis.

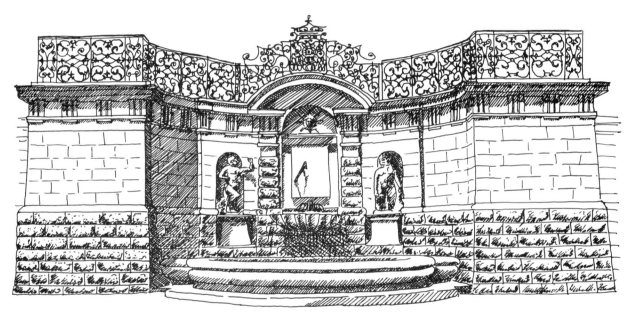

The Perron seen from below.

Away from the formal gardens where the landform has been remodelled, the unaltered valleys and hollows to the north contain two more contrasting and surprising elements. The 'American Gardens' or arboretum was begun by Daniel Robertson to house trees originating from North America and then only just being introduced into Ireland. Today this sheltered valley con-tains some splendid specimens of trees such as spruce and fir, many of them of particularly large size. Their informal layout and the mass/space relationship within the enclosed valley provide a welcome contrast to the formal gardens. The other element is the Japanese garden laid out in 1908, located in another self-contained hollow where a small-scale layout includes bright red painted bridges to give further contrast. It might be expected that this

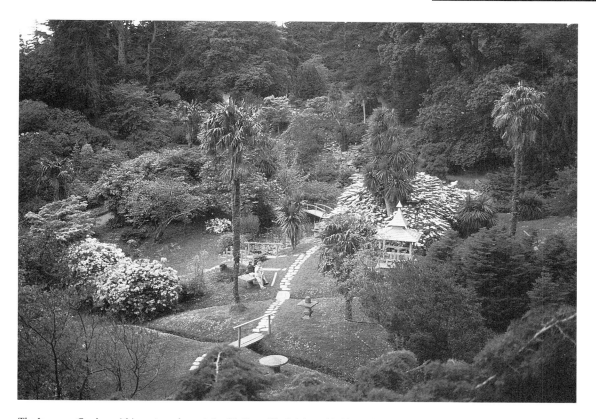

The Japanese Garden within a strongly contained hollow. The bright red bridges add accent colour at dull times of the year.

would be out of place, but because it is visually separated from the formal gardens, and because the visitor has had time to absorb their drama before any of the others they contribute to complementary unity, each emphasizing the other.

A small-scale detail, but a useful focal feature enabling visitors to orientate themselves, is the Pepper-Pot Tower located high on a spur of land overlooking the Arboretum.

At the other side of the formal gardens the landform becomes a plateau or shelf which runs back up towards the house and its associated buildings to the south-west. A strong mass of trees here leads off into a woodland which eventually connects with the landscape beyond the park. The rest of the area comprises formal, walled gardens, some of a more utilitarian nature. The main entrance to the gardens for visitors runs along another axis, this time parallel with the front of the house and leading on to the main terrace. The spaces lead from one to another separated by walls punctuated by elaborate wrought iron gates.

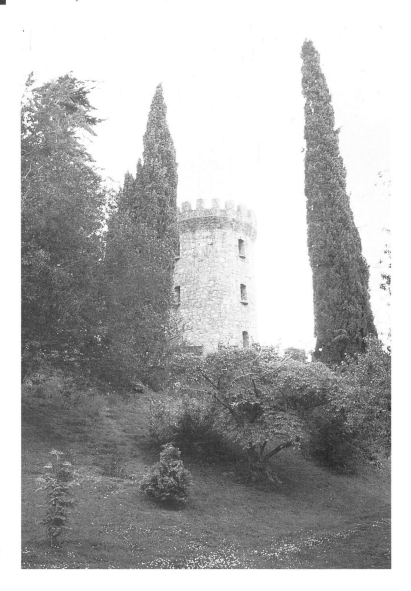

The Pepper Pot Tower flanked by cypresses and positioned on a prominent spur.

One last contrast to the gardens to the south-east is the view to the north-west from the house over a classical 'English parkland' dating from the mid-eighteenth century. The drive into the house and gardens runs through an impressive stand of large beech trees which form a majestic open volume from which glimpses of the park are obtained but no hint of the splendours to be found in the gardens and grounds beyond. Thus the sequence of spaces contained by the built forms and masses of trees reveal by degrees a series of contrasting and varied elements which provide

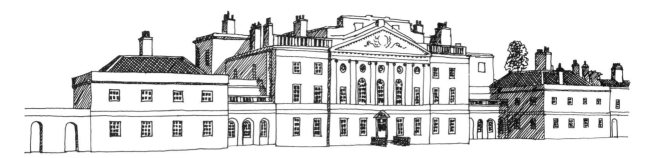

a high degree of variety, constantly tantalizing to the senses yet controlled within a strongly unified structure linked to the world outside. Here is an extensive landscape designed for no other reason than to give pleasure to the senses, developed with a strong sense of continuity yet also satisfying the tastes of the owners of different generations and the prevailing fashions of the day. Once the preserve of the aristocracy, the gardens are now in trust and open to all to enjoy and marvel at the boldness, the scale, the richness and the strong control exerted over the design.

The Palladian front to the house.

Case study 3:
Strathyre Forest, Stirlingshire, Scotland

This case study examines the problem of how to design in a predominantly natural landscape where the objective is to achieve unity between the existing landscape and a man-made and managed plantation forest.

In the years following World War One many thousands of hectares of bare, unforested land in the upland areas of Great Britain were planted with trees to create a reserve of timber in case of another war. Land was purchased and planted with the types of trees which would grow quickly on exposed sites with poor soil. The main trees chosen for this were coniferous, mostly not native to Britain, originating in North America or Europe. As these plantation forests grew up many of them soon began to look awkward, artificial and out of place in the landscape.

There are several reasons for these visual problems. The plantation forest is dark in colour and has a texture very different from the surrounding bare landscape, thus contrasting strongly with it. Such forests were often densely planted with the same species and age of trees so that visual diversity is reduced compared with the vegetation patterns it replaced or with natural forest. Ownership and enclosure patterns have meant that the shapes of these plantations were often strongly geometric, their

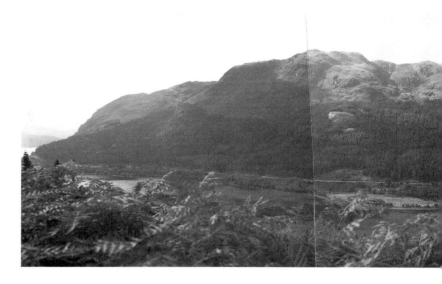

A section of Strathyre Forest before the harvesting began.

impact reinforced by the shadows cast by the trees on the edges. Since many of these forests were planted in mountainous areas where landform is strong and generates many visual forces, visual tensions between the shape of the landform and the forest exacerbate the discordant effect.

Strathyre Forest is an example of one of these early forests suffering from some of the problems described above. Located in a sensitive landscape and visible from a major road for several miles the forest was more or less even-aged although it contained some deciduous trees, mainly larch, which had been planted on former bracken-covered ground and which provided visual diversity in the autumn, winter and spring. The shape of the forest had been determined by the ownership and by an upper planting limit running along a contour line. This produced two predominantly horizontal lines across the slope, top and bottom.

The *genius loci* here is partly derived from the landform, which in this glaciated landscape is strongly modelled on the upper slopes where irregular freeze–thaw action during the Ice Ages was most pronounced and smoother elsewhere owing to direct glacial erosion. The reflection of the back-lit mountains, where the eye is drawn to the skyline, in the still waters of Loch Lubnaig further contributes to the genius. The landform is rhythmical in its shapes and this is picked up by alder and birch along the loch extending up into hollows on the mountainside. None of this modelling was reflected in the design of the first forest. The scale of the forest was better in general terms than many, there being a generous proportion of unplanted (and unplantable) mountain top above the tree line.

The objective of design in these semi-natural landscapes is

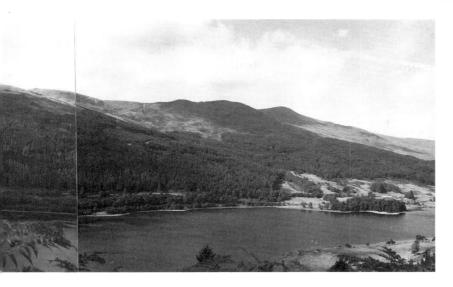

usually to endeavour to blend the forest into its surroundings using appropriate shapes derived from those present in the landform and vegetation patterns, to respond to the visual forces in the landscape and to achieve a good scale relationship between forest and unplanted land and between the different species and ages of trees within the forest. The level of diversity in the forest should reflect that in the surrounding landscape and this should achieve a high level of unity in the overall design if these principles are adhered to. In addition something of the *genius loci* must be incorporated into the design, in order that it does not become 'just another forest'.

One of the first steps in design is to appraise the landscape in order to understand its visual components and to see how the visual patterns so determined are related to site factors. One of the best ways of doing this is to use panoramic photographs or sketches upon which are recorded the various factors. Landform can be analysed using visual forces. Visual problems can be assessed and noted on the sketches. The choice of viewpoint from which to make these assessments is also important.

The main opportunity to redesign the forest occurs at the time that the trees start to be felled for timber. The act of felling enables the existing shape to be remodelled, open space to be created, tree species to be changed and structural diversity in terms of the different ages of trees to be established. This is achieved by felling different parts of the forest at different times, all comprehensively planned to take place over a number of years in sequential fashion.

Since shape is so important, the shapes of the forest are the first and most important elements to design. This includes both the

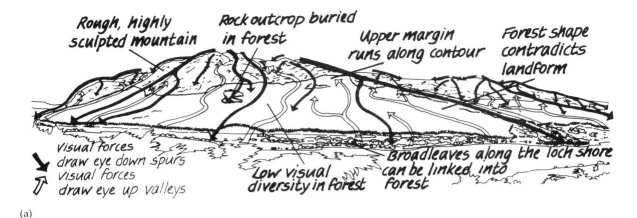

Rough, highly sculpted mountain

Rock outcrop buried in forest

Upper margin runs along contour

Forest shape contradicts landform

Visual forces draw eye down spurs
Visual forces draw eye up valleys

Low visual diversity in forest

Broadleaves along the loch shore can be linked into forest

(a)

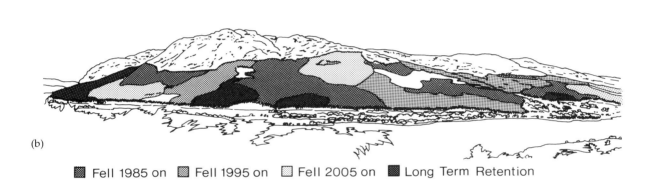

(b)

▨ Fell 1985 on   ▨ Fell 1995 on   ▨ Fell 2005 on   ■ Long Term Retention

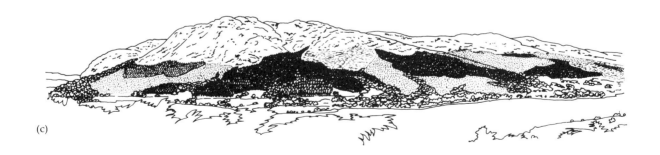

(c)

(a) The visual appraisal which appraises major features of importance in the landscape.
(b) The pattern of interlocking felling coupes. These are larger in scale towards the top of the slope and smaller lower down. Certain stands will be retained for a longer period to maintain stand diversity.
(c) The appearance of the forest at replanting showing how the external margin will be reshaped and how the diversity of the forest will be increased.

192

entire forest in its setting and the individual parts of the forest, be they stands of trees of various ages and species or open space within the forest. The scale of the shapes is the next factor. As we have seen, scale varies with elevation so the shapes of the stands towards the top of the slope should appear larger than those at the bottom. Diversity is ensured by emphasizing the age differences of the stands established by felling and replanting at intervals of up to ten years between adjacent areas, and by the pattern of species – evergreen conifers, deciduous conifers, broadleaved trees and open or unplanted areas.

Unity involves ensuring that the designed shapes are inspired by those present in the landform or vegetation patterns – such as bracken which turns orange/brown in the autumn and winter as does the deciduous conifer, larch. The shapes should interlock with each other which aids unity as does the similarity of shape and the hierarchy of scale down the slope. *Genius loci* should be identified at the initial appraisal stage and the overall design concept should seek to ensure that those qualities are enhanced. At Strathyre the design emphasizes the particular qualities of the landform by ensuring that the strongly modelled rock outcrops are reinforced and exposed to view where previously they have been hidden by trees. Rhythms are introduced into the shapes to reflect those in the landform while the pattern of the broadleaved trees is extended up into the forest.

Particular features of this design are the way in which the upper margin is adjusted by leaving certain spurs bare after felling and by extending the planting further up the gullies than it was originally. All of the visual objectives are achieved within the framework of the functional, physical and economic constraints which exist in these forests, such as the need to fulfil timber market commitments, the limitations of soil and climate on species choice, limitations of logging equipment and access.

Glossary

Accent colour A colour, usually bright, used in small amounts to highlight details and to focus the eye on particular parts of the composition. Often used for doors on large, simple buildings.

Ambient light The level of light present as 'background' at any one time. It casts no shadows. Produced as a result of sunlight redistributed by cloud and atmospheric refraction.

Anthropomorphic Resembling the human body in shape; attributing human characteristics to other things.

Axis A line or linear feature used to organize a composition by drawing the eye in one direction. Used to impart strong structure. Often associated with highly formal or ceremonial designs and with strong authority e.g. church or state.

Background That part of a landscape composition which is furthest from the viewer. Usually this is from five to eight kilometres distant. Details are lost; colours and textures are the main determinants.

Back-lit The lighting condition when an object or landscape is seen with the sun opposite the viewer. Vertical elements are seen in shadow, details are obscured and seen as silhouettes, horizontal surfaces may reflect the light.

Balance A state where all parts of a design or landscape are in equilibrium and no part needs to be moved, added or subtracted.

Bilateral symmetry An arrangement of two elements so that each is the mirror image of the other, reflected across a line or axis.

Building line The line determined by architects, urban designers or planners behind which buildings must be kept. Often found in old towns in order to retain space/mass character, or to allow correct amounts of light to reach the ground.

Chaos That state in which there is, or appears to be, a complete lack of organization or pattern in a scene. Our eyes and brain constantly seek meaningful patterns out of apparent chaos.

Character The distinguishing aspects of an element, a design or a landscape. No value or judgement on a given character need be applied.

Characteristic An element or feature which is repeated or distributed in a design or landscape which is distinctive in itself or contributes to the character of the landscape.

Chroma The strength or saturation of a colour, especially used in reference to the Munsell system of colour classification.

Clear-cut An area of forest or woodland where all the trees are felled or cleared within a short space of time. This normally results in high colour and textural contrast with the surrounding forest.

Coalescence When several elements overlap each other or otherwise interrupt a clear view of any one of them then they are said to coalesce visually. A technique used to create the appearance of greater scale using a number of small elements.

Colour The characteristic of a material which affects the way light is reflected from it. Colour is used to describe the section of the visible spectrum which is reflected by a surface, all the other sections being absorbed by the surface.

Colour circle A method of arranging primary, secondary and tertiary colours, according to a spectral relationship in a complete circle.

Complementary colours Pairs of colours which when mixed produce white light. Colours found opposite each other on the colour circle; colours which produce an after-image of each other.

Component   An identifiable part of a composition or design, often comprising a subsidiary composition as part of the whole, with its own characteristics.

Composition   A collection of different elements or components arranged in such a way as to create a satisfying and identifiable whole. In the landscape, compositions may be identified as landform units without a conscious act of design being involved.

Continuity   The sense of a pattern or landscape extending as a similar character over space or time; the use of repeated elements or characteristics in a design or their occurrence in nature.

Contour   An imaginary line described on a map or plan linking points of identical height above a datum or bench mark. Frequently used to determine the shape or position of real lines such as roads on the landscape.

Contrapuntal   The simultaneous existence of two rhythms either at a different speed or in different directions but which harmonize (see counterpoint).

Contrast   The visible difference between two elements or parts of a design when seen close together. The greater the differences and the closer the position, the greater the contrast.

Corinthian Order   The third order of classical Greek architecture, characterized by fluted columns and Acanthus-leaved capitols and certain other features in the ornamentation.

Counterpoint   The conscious use of opposing characteristics in a design in order to achieve a more lively end result. Often found in rhythm (similar concept to musical counterpoint) or in asymmetric balance.

Curvilinear   A line or edge of a plane, which is characterized by a smoothly curving shape lacking angles or straight sections.

Datum   A point, line, plane or volume used to organize elements in space by virtue of their location or position in relation to it.

Dendritic   A pattern of river drainage where the streams resemble the branches of a tree. (Ancient Greek *Dendros* = tree.)

Density   The relative visual solidity of a pattern e.g. in amounts of tree cover. Density is best appreciated when gradual changes from one degree to another occur.

Direction   A description of the position or location of elements which lead the eye from one part of a composition to another.

Disruptive   Anything in a design or composition which tends to detract from visual unity; often the lack of one of the factors which help to organize a design.

Diversity   The degree or amount of variety in a design or landscape. Recognized as an important attribute of a good design but subject to diminishing return if taken too far.

Dominance   The apparently greater strength or importance of one factor in a composition. Often a useful way to establish a logical order or hierarchy in a design.

Doric Order   The first order of classical Greek architecture featuring fluted columns and a plain base and capital.

Dualistic symmetry   The repetition or reflection of almost similar elements, particularly where shape is the same but colours or textures are substituted.

Element   One of the basic building blocks of a composition: point, line, plane, or volume.

Enclosure   The partial enclosing of a volume or space with one or more elements to suggest a larger element. Used to create the illusion of greater scale with small-sized elements.

Equilibrium   The state where all the parts of a composition or design are in balance with one another; where all visual forces and tension are resolved.

Euclidean geometry   The spatial description of regular planes and solids recognized by the ancient Greeks.

Fenestration   The pattern made by windows in the façade of a building. Often contributes to scale, proportion and diversity in architecture.

Fibonacci series   A numbering system in which the next number in the series is found by the addition of the two preceding ones. The series can be used to create a logarithmic spiral such as that found in plant and animal growth.

Figure   Any feature, usually of high contrast, which stands out from its surroundings or background. The eye is usually drawn to such features.

Foreground   The nearest part of a view in which details of individual features such as plants, stones, textures etc, are visible. Extends up to half a kilometre from the observer.

Form   The three-dimensional equivalent of shape.

Front-lit   The appearance of a scene when the light source is behind the observer. The landscape appears flat but details, especially colours, appear clear.

Genius loci   The intangible qualities which contribute to the identity of a place and help determine the differences between one place and another.

Geodesic   A method of construction using regular stable geometric shapes such as triangles or hexagons which interconnect to form strong structures requiring little internal support.

Geometric   A description of shape derived from that branch of mathematics, usually simple and regular, comprising straight lines, right angles, arcs of circles etc.

Golden section   A rule or theory of proportion determined by the proportion of 1:1.618 and seen in a rectangle of those proportions. Used extensively in art and in classical architecture.

Grain   A description of texture when applied to more distant scenes e.g. background views where major patterns in a landscape are seen as such. Often has directional qualities.

Hierarchy   A method of ordering sections of a composition so that some parts are more important or dominant than others. Size, scale, position, colour etc, can be used to determine hierarchy.

Horizon   The line where sky and land appear to meet.

Hue   The attribute or description by which one colour is distinguished from another e.g. red, blue, green. A specific descriptor of the Munsell system.

Interlock   A relationship between two elements where one extends into or interpenetrates another. Characterized by increased edge length and an enhanced visual connection between them.

Interval   The spacing between elements in space or time.

Ionic order   The second order of Greek architecture featuring smooth columns and distinctive 'ram's horns' on the capital.

Jeffersonian Grid   The name commonly given to the land survey and organization carried out as colonization proceeded from east to west in the USA.

Kaleidoscopic symmetry   The repetition of identical elements arranged with several planes or lines over which they can be divided. Commonly seen in patterns of equal segments arranged in a circle.

Light   The visible part of the spectrum of electromagnetic radiation given out by the sun or artificial sources by which we can see our surroundings.

Line   A basic element dominated by one dimension. May be an extended point, a long narrow feature or the edge of a plane.

Mass   Solid volume, usually perceived as a contrast to open space.

Middle ground   That part of a scene between the foreground and the background, usually between one to six kilometres distant. Shape and form are evident but surface detail becomes lost.

Modulor   A system of proportion derived by the architect Le Corbusier and based on the proportions of the human body.

Moiré effect   An optical illusion of movement produced by the arrangement of shapes and colours. The effect can be quite unnerving and can appear to change as we shift focus. Moiré patterns are commonly caused by visual interference of two sets of line screens in printing.

Monochrome   A composition where tones, tints and shades of the one colour only are used. Commonly refers to shades of grey or to black-and-white photographs of the landscape.

Munsell system   A method of describing colour devised by Alfred Munsell in 1915, dividing colours into three variables, hue, chroma and value. Widely used by colourists and in the choice of colour e.g. by the British Standards Institution.

Naturalistic   The appearance of being natural; the description of a landscape designed to appear natural as perceived or understood by particular people.

Nearness   The proximity of elements in space such that they appear to be part of a group in a composition.

Number   The presence of more than one element. As number increases a design or composition can become increasingly complex and visually confused.

Organic   An attribute of shape and form where the plane or volume resembles natural shapes, especially those of plants or animals; usually highly asymmetric, often diffuse and ill-defined at the edges.

Orientation   The position of an element in relation to a particular compass direction, the observer or some other factor e.g. wind or sun direction. Literally 'facing east'.

Palimpsest   The history of a place which can be read from the accumulated remains left behind. Obvious in places with a history of long habitation. Derived from the ancient practice of re-using parchment where traces of the former text were left behind and written over.

Palladian   A style of architecture founded by the Italian renaissance architect Andrea Palladio. Picked up in eighteenth century Europe. Characterized by well-proportioned, symmetrical composition in the classical manner.

Palette The selection of colours used by an artist in a painting; the colours used in a given design or composition; the range of colours which characterize a particular landscape.

Perception The activity carried out by the brain by which we interpret what the senses (mainly sight for most people) receive. It is not merely a factual reporting but tends to be referenced to associations and expectations already present in the mind of the beholder.

Pergola A frame of uprights and cross-pieces used to train plants to create an enclosed space in a garden or park.

Perron A feature combining steps and fountains used to change levels in terraced gardens. A notable example is at Powerscourt in Ireland.

Picture plane That implied plane which forms the boundary of the space depicted in a painting or photograph and the real world. Perspective may be designed to continue from the real world into the painting to create the illusion that the picture is real (*trompe l'oeil*).

Pilaster A partial column set against a wall which appears to aid support of part of a building in classical architecture. Used to break up a façade and to introduce scale and proportion as well as decoration.

Plane A basic element where two dimensions dominate. It may be flat, curved, real or implied. It may be a roof or wall but more commonly the floor or ground plane.

Point A basic element of very small dimension relative to the scale or size of the composition. Position and number are important.

Pointilliste A style of art practised by certain members of the Impressionist school such as Seurat where the painting is composed of very small dots of pure colour. At the distance from which the picture is seen the eye blends the dots into a range of colours not actually present in the painting.

Position The location of an element in space and often with reference to another element or a plane such as the ground.

Proportion The relationship of parts of a design or composition to the whole, especially in size or degree. Various rules or theories of proportion have been established from ancient times.

Quincunx An arrangement of five points to make a cross with a centre. Used to arrange e.g. five plants in a bed, five trees without the regularity of 4 or 6 in number.

Rhythm The repetition of similar elements at the same or related intervals so that they appear to be part of a whole composition and create an illusion of movement. Rhythm increases interest and introduces dynamics into a design.

Rule of thirds A way of proportioning parts of a design by dividing it into sections of one third to two thirds of the whole. Loosely based on the Golden Section it helps achieve a hierarchical balance in which one part dominates.

Scale The size of elements in relation to the human body and to the landscape. Scale varies with the position and distance of the observer.

Shape The attribute of a plane in the way its edges are varied. Shapes can be geometric or irregular. A most important variable.

Shell roof A form of construction where a thin shell of e.g. concrete is used to create a form utilizing the strength properties of the egg shell. Organic or irregular forms can be created using this method.

Side-lit The landscape seen when the light comes from the side of the observer is side-lit. Three-dimensional form and texture are emphasized but colour is also visible. A good condition for appraising the landscape.

Similarity The degree to which elements resemble each other in their visual characteristics. We tend to link similar elements together visually.

Size The degree of variation in dimensions of various elements. Large sizes impress us. Size can be used to create diversity. Size and scale interact.

Space-frame A construction, usually of interconnecting tubular sections, which is used to create partial space, often outside.

Spatial cues Those principles of organization which refer to the visual interaction of positions of elements, such as nearness, enclosure, interlock, similarity.

Spirit of place See *Genius loci*.

Structural elements Those principles of organization used to confer a structure to a composition, such as rhythm, tension, balance, proportion and scale.

Symmetry The arrangement of elements so that one part of a composition is balanced by an identical or mirror image in another part.

Tactile The sensation of touch;

perception of the world by touch alone. Textures may be tactile as well as visual.

Tension The interaction of visual forces which can create conflict but which, when resolved, can introduce greater interest in a design.

Texture The visual or tactile quality of a surface introduced by numerous repeated elements. The size and interval of the elements determines the degree of coarseness or fineness of the texture.

Time The fourth dimension; the landscape changes over various time intervals – short term to long term, daily, seasonally or over many years.

Top-lit When the lighting direction is above the observer the landscape is top-lit. Few shadows except beneath objects. Occurs in lower latitudes.

Transformation The gradual change in a landscape or design over space and time.

Tree line The line or zone where tree growth ceases owing to climatic effects found at high altitudes or high latitudes. May be quite abrupt.

Unity The appearance of wholeness or completeness and continuity in a design or landscape; the organization of elements to produce a clearly identifiable composition.

Value The lightness or darkness of a colour. The third variable described under the Munsell system.

Visible spectrum That part of the electromagnetic spectrum which we can see as coloured or white light.

Visual force The illusion of movement, or potential movement found in a static image or object. The landscape is full of visual forces, especially influencing the way we look at landform.

Visual inertia The attribute of an element which is extremely stable and inert. Usually horizontal in emphasis.

Volume The basic element where all three spatial dimensions are present. Can be perceived as solid volumes – seen as a mass from outside – or as open volumes – seen as a space from inside.

— References and Further — Reading

Since one of the reasons for writing this book is the dearth of material on the subject, any reference list is likely to be somewhat meagre. Instead of merely listing a number of books in the usual way it will be more useful to readers if they are presented with a selected, critical bibliography containing some comment on the scope and value of the books contained in it. Cervantes, the sixteenth-century Spanish writer, castigated authors who merely copy out a long list of references culled from other works in order to lend authority to their own work. Each of the books mentioned here contains its own reference list. Readers who consult any of them will be able to delve further back into its sources. Since a number of books cited here date back some years, their references date back further, are often out of print and are certainly hard to come by.

Recent books have tended to concentrate on specific aspects of design in greater depth than can be covered by this volume. Colour is one area particularly well represented, and the subjects of forest landscape design, garden design, and the works of famous designers and architects have also been popular topics in recent years.

Here is a selected bibliography presented in categories of subject areas. The comments on them are entirely the author's own.

Aesthetics and design principles

CHING, F.D.K. (1979) *Architecture: Form, Space and Order*, Van Nostrand Reinhold, New York.

This is a useful text set out in a clear, pictorial way. It applies many of the design principles, but is only concerned with built form. The examples are drawn from a wide source and are clearly illustrated. It is a little difficult to find one's way about the structure of the book if one dips into it or wishes to find a specific section.

GARRETT, L. (1967) *Visual Design: a problem solving approach*, Van Nostrand Reinhold, New York.

A seminal work looking at design principles based on the relationship between creation in nature and art. Aimed at graphic designers, the book is intended to stimulate creativity. While some of the examples are a little dated, it is, nevertheless, a highly original work.

GOMBRICH, E.H. (1982) *The Image and the Eye*, Phaidon Press, Oxford.

This work is a series of collected essays on art and visual perception. It is one of a number by this author on the same subject. They deal with the psychology of perception – how we see what we see and some of the ways our perception is affected by other factors – optical illusion, cultural conventions and the like. While mainly related to art, it is also useful for designers, particularly anyone trying to come to terms with appearances and reality.

JACKOBSEN, P. (1977) Shrubs and ground cover, in *Landscape Design with Plants* (ed. B. Clouston), Heinemann, London.

Although dealing mainly with planting design, the section deals very well with a number of visual design principles – scale, proportion, ordering, balance – and their application in smaller garden or park landscapes. Presented using sketches, diagrams and photos the emphasis is on fairly formal, sculptural uses of shrubs and ground-cover.

LEONHARDT, F. (1982) *Brucken/Bridges*, Architectural Press, London.

This fascinating book on the subject of bridge design also has an interesting section on aesthetics written by an engineer. The section considers the nature of aesthetics, how we perceive aesthetics and the place of taste, among other things. The book goes on to explore bridge construction with aesthetics as much in mind as function and cost.

McCLUSKEY, J. (1985) Principles of design, in *Landscape Design* Nos 153–158 (ed. K. Fieldhouse), London.

A series of articles dealing with aesthetic principles in the landscape presented using diagrams, sketches and photographs. The short series is not able to deal in depth with each of the aspects considered. Much is a synthesis of previous work. Since the series is split between issues there is some loss of continuity between each section and occasionally confusion creeps in over the precise application of a principle.

DE SAUSMAREZ, M. (1964) *Basic Design: the dynamics of visual form*, Studio Vista, London/Van Nostrand Reinhold, New York.

A slim volume providing a clear introduction to the basis of fine art, exploring the elements of pictorial expression and the dynamic forces contained in them. Illustrated using abstract and real examples, the reader is invited to apply the basic principles using analytical drawings, and to find out for himself the dynamics and processes underlying visual expression.

Colour

BIRREN, F. (1969) *Principles of Colour*, Van Nostrand Reinhold, New York.
Subtitled *A review of past traditions and modern theories of colour harmony*, this work is an elementary introduction to the subject. It suffers from being mainly in black and white, with the short colour sections to be found at the back of the book making it somewhat difficult to read. The text is well organized, explaining the basic principles of colour and their relationships, although their application is barely touched on.

LANCASTER, M. (1984) *Britain in View*, Quiller Press, London.
A very interesting and stimulating book which deals first with the description and principles of colour and then analyses Britain in terms of the colours found in the landscape and their traditional uses. There follows a section applying colour theory to a variety of circumstances – gardens, farming, industry, power etc. Well presented and produced although large sections are, of course, only applicable to Britain.

PORTER, T. (1982) *Colour Outside*, The Architectural Press, London.
A book looking almost exclusively at architectural uses of colour. The author nevertheless deals in an exciting way with a variety of possibilities and is able to emphasize the importance of colour. One particular strength is the explanation of various methods of applying the principles of colour such as those of the French colourist Jean-Phillipe Lenclos. Some of the examples are now a little dated since the use of colour in urban settings is prone to changes of taste and fashion.

Genius loci

DAVIES, P. and KNIPE, A. (1984) *A Sense of Place: sculpture in the landscape*, Ceolfrith Press, Sunderland.
A fascinating look at the use of sculpture in various settings to draw out and reflect the *genius loci*. The work of a number of sculptors is examined, some particularly interested in the use of natural materials and some interested in ephemeral effects. Some of the sculptures are pieces set in landscapes, others are part of the landscape itself.

DRABBLE, M. (1979) *A Writer's Britain*, Thames and Hudson, London.
A wide-ranging look at how writers have observed and described Britain over several centuries. It reveals a changing attitude to the landscape and shows how many writers, particularly novelists and poets, can get to the heart of the *genius loci* in a most memorable way.

HARDY, T. (1878) *The Return of the Native*, Macmillan, London.
Thomas Hardy, whatever the shortcomings of the plots of his novels, is a superb describer of the landscapes in which his characters live. One of the greatest evocations of the spirit of a landscape occurs in the opening chapter of *The Return of the Native,* an atmospheric characterization of the Dorset heaths of the south of England. Other novels contain similar passages.

NORBERG-SCHULZ, C. (1980) *Genius loci*, Academy Editions, London.
    This is a book devoted to the identification and understanding of 'place' in architecture and, to some extent, the landscape. It is wide-ranging in its coverage of the sources of *genius loci* – the cultural, the symbolic – and what gives character to more extensive areas. Following a discussion of place in natural environments some case studies, all urban, are examined in detail. One of the problems of the book is that it is difficult to penetrate owing to the layout and lack of headings and subtitles to help the reader find his way about.

Landscapes and landscape design

COLVIN, B. (1970) *Land and Landscape*, 2nd edn, John Murray, London.
    This now classic work traces three themes, according to its subtitle: *evolution, design and control*. In it, Brenda Colvin follows landscape development in Britain from early to modern times. She follows this with a section on various design principles, especially related to land use and then in a whole range of practical situations such as climatic conditions. There follows a look at design in practice categorized by general landscape types. Amply illustrated in black and white the book is now 20 years old but much of what Brenda Colvin says is dateless and helps put some of the patterns and design solutions into their context.

CROWE, DAME SYLVIA (1981) *Garden Design*, 2nd edn, Packard Publishing in association with Thomas Gibson Publishing, London.
    In this work restricted to the landscape of gardens, albeit some of them quite large, Sylvia Crowe looks first at garden history, then a set of design principles to apply to the handling of mass and space and composition. Following this she looks at the use of materials and finishes with a study of specialized gardens. The logic and sequence of the work is similar to Colvin, cited above, but covers different ground. One strong aspect of the book is that it shows that garden design, like all else, is primarily about composition, and not the details of individual plants.

CROWE, DAME SYLVIA and MITCHELL, M. (1988) *The pattern of landscape*, Packard Publishing, Chichester.
    This work traces the links between the physical functioning of the earth's surface and the responses it evokes in men. It uses three themes: the nature of landscape, the landscape as a habitat and the human response to show how the dynamic patterns of the landscape and man's activities are related and can result in harmony or destruction. Profusely illustrated, it is a testament to the deep understanding gained by the authors over many years. It is, however, a broad and challenging look rather than a deep and detailed examination.

FAIRBROTHER, N. (1970) *New Lives, New Landscapes*, Architectural Press, London.
    This is more of a manifesto than a book on landscape. In this influential work the author shows how British society has changed yet

occupies an old setting. From this she looks at what kind of landscapes are required for this newly emerged society and from this she presents a four-point plan for a new landscape framework and examines ways of achieving it. Since the book was written the landscape of the British countryside and city have continued to change, as has society, in many ways quite dramatically, but the central message is still relevant though the plan itself is perhaps dated.

FAIRBROTHER, N. (1974) *The Nature of Landscape Design*, Architectural Press, London.

The second of the two agenda-setting books, this loses nothing by being 17 years old. The examination of what design is all about, its connection with nature and the need to understand the dynamic aspect of the landscape are woven together in an extremely readable way. It is a book which enthuses the reader but, perhaps, leaves him or her a little bewildered as to what to do next. It is a missionary work.

JELLICOE, SIR GEOFFREY (1970) *Studies in Landscape Design*, Oxford University Press, Oxford.

In this three-volume series Geoffrey Jellicoe examines a wide range of landscapes, some designed, others not, and looks at the inspiration behind them, their history and composition to blend the cultural, symbolic and aesthetic aspects into one. Each chapter has a theme or subject area to act as a lens through which each is viewed: for example, 'The Landscape of Symbols'. Once again, the work is some 20 years old and there is much new design worth examining in the same way. Emerging from the work is the feeling that Jellicoe is able to tap into the *genius loci* of each of his examples and show how 'place' can be established.

JELLICOE, SIR GEOFFREY (1987) *The Landscape of Man*, 2nd edn, Thames and Hudson, London.

This major work explores the interaction of man and his surroundings over many centuries since civilization began. The author looks at the way different cultures and their values, political systems and cultural symbols interact with the landscape. He shows how the designs created in different periods reflect all those factors. The book is well structured, taking each country or period and relating its setting, background and environment before examining the major results in terms of landscape and architecture. A massive work, authoritatively presented and an important contribution to an understanding of our place in the world.

SIMMONDS, J.O. (1961) *Landscape Architecture*, Iliffe Books, London.

This book, subtitled *The shaping of man's environment*, looks at many of the visual design principles related to living spaces in the landscape, and their application, not only visually but symbolically and in terms of some of the emotions aroused by shape, scale, different spaces and ways of organizing the environment.

Ecology and design

FORMAN, R.T.T. and GORDON, M. (1986) *Landscape Ecology*, Wiley, New York.

This book makes a major contribution to the understanding of the landscape as a series of patterns seen at different scales. Although approached from an ecological perspective it has real value since the patterns can be understood both visually, and also in the context of the ecological processes at work. The analysis is conveyed through a number of case studies and examples at various scales and in various locations. Where the book fails is on the question of how to make use of this understanding in design.

McHARG, I. (1969) *Design with Nature*, Natural History Press, New York.

This is another of those seminal works which changed the way people thought about the landscape. As a means of understanding the landscape and using that knowledge to inform planning and design it has never been surpassed. It is, however, an analytical approach which tends to assume that design synthesis somehow occurs spontaneously as a result of the analysis.

Forest design

ANSTEY, C., THOMPSON, S. and NICHOLS, K. (1982) *Creative Forestry*, New Zealand Forest Service, Wellington.

This volume explores the variety of forested landscapes of New Zealand, looks at some principles of design and considers how they might be applied in the context of the management and exploitation of the forest. Well presented, using graphics and photographs, it suffers from a lack of demonstrable examples of the principles at work and from a slightly over-simplistic presentation of the basic principles themselves.

FORESTRY COMMISSION OF TASMANIA (1990) *A Manual for Forest Landscape Management*, Forestry Commission of Tasmania, Hobart.

A recently produced handsome publication based largely on the principles and practice of the US Forest Service as applied to the Tasmanian landscape. It suffers from the same shortcomings as the US Forest Service methods (see below). It contains a useful assessment of the different landscape character types of the state but falls short of showing how the principles previously described can be applied to each type.

LITTON, R.B.Jnr (1968) *Forest Landscape Description and Inventories*, USDA Forest Service Research Paper PSW-49, USDA, Washington DC.

This is a handy, short book which provides a useful framework for describing and categorizing a landscape. In particular, it attempts to consider the interactions between the perception of the landscape – scale, for example, with the position of the observer. It also provides a useful categorization of landscapes into morphological types.

Lucas, O.W.R. (1991) *The Design of Forest Landscapes*, Oxford University Press, Oxford.

This is a major work demonstrating the principles and practice of forest landscape design in a wide-ranging way using lots of examples taken from actual practice. The strength of the approach lies in the more detailed understanding of visual design principles and their application to a comprehensive range of forestry activities, all of which are tried and tested and proven to work. A further strength is the use of the principles to design to quite a high resolution of detail compared with other works on the subject. The book is also extremely well presented.

Province of British Columbia (1981) *Forest Landscape Handbook*, Ministry of Forests, Victoria, BC.

Another publication based on the US Forest Service system, this time applied to the circumstances in British Columbia. It suffers the same problems as its inspiration.

US Dept of Agriculture Forest Service (1973) *National Forest Landscape Management*, Vol 1, USDA Forest Service, Washington DC.

This is the first in a series of publications dealing with the management of forest landscapes. Volume 1 explores a number of design principles and illustrates them using photographs and diagrams. It seeks to show how aspects of landscape change can be fitted into natural landscapes. One drawback is the limited range of principles examined and some confusion over their categorization and interpretation. Subsequent volumes apply the principles in the context of the visual management system. The major problem with this series is that it enables activities to be planned so that apparent landscape change is minimized but it fails to tackle the application of the principles to creative design.

Index